S1 SEP 2015
D0172914

INSIGHT

EXPLORE

RIO DE JANEIRO

⦿ Walking Eye App

Your Insight Guide purchase includes a free download of the destination's corresponding eBook. It is available now from the free Walking Eye container app in the App Store and Google Play. Simply download the Walking Eye container app to access the eBook dedicated to your purchased book. The app also features free information on local events taking place and activities you can enjoy during your stay, with the option to book them. In addition, premium content for a wide range of other destinations is available to purchase in-app.

HOW TO DOWNLOAD THE WALKING EYE APP

Available on purchase of this guide only.
1. Visit our website: www.insightguides.com/walkingeye
2. Download the Walking Eye container app to your smartphone (this will give you access to your free eBook and the ability to purchase other products)
3. Select the scanning module in the Walking Eye container app
4. Scan the QR Code on this page – you will be asked to enter a verification word from the book as proof of purchase
5. Download your free eBook* for travel information on the go

* Other destination apps and eBooks are available for purchase separately or are free with the purchase of the Insight Guide book

CONTENTS

Introduction

Recommended Routes for...   6
Explore Rio de Janeiro   10
Food and Drink   16
Shopping   20
Entertainment   22
History: Key Dates   24

Directory

Accommodations   96
Restaurants   104
Nightlife   114
A–Z   116
Language   130
Books and Film   134

Credits

About This Book   136
Credits   137
Index   138

Best Routes

1. Sugarloaf and Praia Vermelha   28
2. Corcovado and Christ the Redeemer   33
3. Botanic Gardens   38
4. Santa Teresa   44
5. Botafogo   49
6. The Centro: Rio's Downtown   55
7. Cinelândia and Lapa   61
8. Copacabana   66
9. Ipanema and Lagoa   72
10. Zona Norte   78
11. Niterói   83
12. Paquetá Island and Guanabara Bay   89

ART BUFFS

Discover naïve art at the base of Corcovado (route 2); take a tram up to Santa Teresa to see fine art in the Chácara do Ceu (route 4); and spend time in the art museums and churches of Downtown Rio (routes 6 and 7).

RECOMMENDED ROUTES FOR...

BACK TO NATURE

Explore the tropical gardens of the Jardim Botânico (route 3); sit on a cog train as you head through rainforest up Corcovado (route 2); and set off on a quiet hiking trail at the end of Copacabana Beach (route 8).

HISTORY BUFFS

Walk the cobbled streets of Rio's Downtown (routes 6 and 7), with colonial churches, a former aqueduct and an imperial palace; see Rio's series of coastal forts (routes 8 and 11); and visit the home of a 19th-century politician (route 5).

MUSIC LOVERS

Discover different genres of live music from Northeast Brazil in a buzzing atmosphere (route 10); sit in a bar listening to samba bands (route 7); and learn about the classical music composer, Villa-Lobos (route 5).

RAINY DAYS

Head to the ornate Municipal Theater and National Library (route 7) and four impressive museums (route 6), or spend time in a pavillion with food stalls and music from Northeast Brazil (route 10).

SEASIDE FUN

Check out Rio's iconic beaches, including Copacabana (route 8) and Ipanema (route 9); head across Guanabara Bay to laid-back Niterói (route 11); and spend a relaxing day on charming Paquetá Island (route 12).

SPECTACULAR VIEWS

Take the cable car up the Sugarloaf (route 1), the cog train up to Christ the Redeemer (route 2) and a gondola over a sprawling favela (route 10), then photograph Rio's mountain peaks from across Guanabara Bay (route 11).

VILLAS AND GARDENS

Learn about orchids and Amazonian trees in Rio's Botanic Gardens (route 3); see the landscaped grounds and palace of Parque Lage (route 9); and check out the old-fashioned manor houses of Santa Teresa (route 4).

INTRODUCTION

An introduction to Rio de Janeiro's geography, customs and culture, plus illuminating background information on cuisine, history and what to do when you're there.

Explore Rio de Janeiro	10
Food and Drink	16
Shopping	20
Entertainment	22
History: Key Dates	24

View over Rio from Sugarloaf Mountain

EXPLORE RIO DE JANEIRO

Situated on picturesque Guanabara Bay, and boasting immense wonders of both the natural and artificial variety, it's no wonder visitors flock from all over the world to experience Rio de Janeiro.

When Rio de Janeiro started out as a tiny European settlement, few would have guessed that one day it would grow into one of the most popular tourist destinations in all of Latin America. The city covers some 485 sq miles (780 sq km), within which hilly tropical forests slope down into concrete jungles that stretch all the way to the coast, where turquoise waters lap at the shores while armies of scantily clad bronzed bodies play in the surf. Views from landmarks such as Christ the Redeemer and the Sugarloaf allow visitors to survey the action, but it's on the ground where the true *carioca* experience is had. The pulse of the city is found in the heat, the beaches, the music, the dance, and the party to end all parties: Carnival.

rainforest. The peaks, which include the famous Sugarloaf (Pão de Açúcar), Corcovado, Dois Irmãos and flat-topped Gávea, dramatically hug the sea and give Rio its signature beauty. Rio is lined with some 90km (56 miles) of beaches, and nearly one-fifth of the city is tropical forest. A staggering number of bus routes, as well as an efficient metro system, connect residents from every end of the city.

The naming of Rio de Janeiro was based on a misunderstanding. A popular version says Gonçalo Coelho, the Portuguese navigator who first reached Guanabara Bay, mistakenly thought it was the mouth of a great river. He looked at his calendar and proclaimed it the 'River of January' (Rio de Janeiro in Portuguese).

GEOGRAPHY AND LAYOUT

Rio lies on the Atlantic Ocean, somewhat more than halfway down Brazil's eastern coast and very nearly smack on the Tropic of Capricorn. The coastal mountain ranges consist of granite peaks draped in lush tropical

HISTORY AND ARCHITECTURE

Rio de Janeiro may have started out as simple settlement in the 16th century, but by the 1700s it had become the country's capital (mostly due to its proximity to gold and diamond mines). Even the Portuguese royal family, in a

Carnival parade

gambit to escape Napoleon's armies, relocated to Rio, leaving Dom João of Portugal, the Queen's son, to act as regent. Thus he became the only monarch in history to rule a European country from a colony. It was under his reign that Brazil abolished slavery in 1888. One year later the monarch himself was ousted, and Brazil was declared a federal republic. The 20th century saw further growth until the capital was moved to Brasilia in 1960. Despite the shift in power, Rio continued to prosper, and now the city is a prominent fixture on the global stage.

Not so surprisingly, Rio wears its colonial history on its sleeve. The greatest concentration of historic monuments and colonial architecture lies near the Praça Quinze de Novembro (Fifteenth of November Square), the very heart of the old city. There, you'll find landmarks, such as the Ingreja de Candelaria, which feature a mix of Baroque and neoclassical styles. However, in this same neighborhood you'll also find monuments to god that are examples of artistic expression, like the 80-meter (263ft) -high, conical-shaped Catedral Metropolitana.

But architecture aficionados needn't look only to the past to find interesting examples. Across Guanabara Bay lies the city of Niteroí, at the edge of which sits the Museu de Arte Contemporânea (see page 86), referred to by many as the 'spaceship' due to its unique flying-saucer-like design. Famed Brazilian

History of Carnival

Until the middle of the 19th century, Carnival in Rio was an aimless and often unseemly outbreak of water fights and practical jokes, derived from Portuguese tradition. In 1855 a band of young men donned colorful costumes and marched to music before an elite audience, including the emperor. The idea caught fire with the public, other groups were formed, and special marches were composed for the bands. Soon the music evolved into Brazilian forms of light-hearted *choros* and somber *ranchos*. After World War I, the pace picked up with the invention of the musical form samba, and the groups of revelers became bigger and better disciplined.

The modern era began in 1928 with the organization of the first *escola de samba* – not a school at all, but a confraternity of Carnival celebrants united in their dedication to perfecting the music, dancing, costumes and floats. Several more *escolas* soon followed, and by 1933 a formal jury had been established to select the parade's best group.

Ever since, competition for Carnival honors has been every bit as exciting to the *cariocas* as soccer's World Cup, and the locals have become as passionate about supporting their 'school' of choice as they are about their soccer teams.

Fashionistas in Ipanema

architect Oscar Niemeyer designed the building, and it was completed in 1996. The structure allows for full panoramic views of Rio de Janeiro across the bay, and to this day it remains a landmark destination for visitors to Rio.

CLIMATE

Rio is about as close to the equator as Havana, Cuba, so winter is a mere formality. In July (the worst of winter south of the equator), the average temperature dips to only 69°F (20°C). This scarcely interferes with the outdoor way of life; the beaches are crowded most of the year. While summer, which runs from late December to late March, brings the *cariocas* to the beaches in unrelenting waves, it can be frighteningly hot and humid for wintering travelers from northern Europe and North America. When the weather begins to heat up around October, it's a sign for *cariocas* that Carnival is on its way.

The allure of Carnival not withstanding, the best times to travel to Rio to avoid the crowds are April to October. The weather is cooler but never cold, the beaches are still populated, and the summer haze clears. Visitors from the northern hemisphere who come in January usually resist the idea of using a beach umbrella at that time of year, but the afternoon sun during Rio's summer is extremely intense. Make sure you apply sun block gener-

ously. In any season, be sure to drink plenty of liquids. Rio's abundant natural juice bars are perfect for pit stops. Above all, take it easy on the beach if you arrive in scorching summer, when it's not unusual to have a string of 90°F (32°C) days with 90 percent humidity. The driest months of the year are May to October, a time when the temperature is lower and you may actually see some sweaters.

THE PEOPLE

Rarely has the term 'multi-ethnic' been more apt than where it concerns Brazilians, *cariocas* in particular. Like many other countries colonized by Europeans, Brazil's track record of dealing with indigenous peoples isn't a very distinguished one. The original inhabitants of Brazil were Indians, whom the Portuguese enslaved. Today, about a third of Brazilians are *mestiços*, of mixed Portuguese and Indian origin. Slightly more than half are white or predominantly white, and Afro-Brazilians make up just over 10 percent of the population. Music, religion, sport and language have all benefited from the intermingling of peoples in Brazil, and this can be seen and felt on the streets of Rio. To this end, Brazilians achieved a remarkable level of racial harmony. However, economic racism is endemic in Brazil. It can be seen first-hand in the city, where tiers of favelas sit alongside

Rocinha favela residents   *Volleyball on the beach*

DON'T LEAVE RIO WITHOUT...

Walking the brightly colored steps of Lapa. Escadaria Selarón, known simply as 'the steps', is the most colorful part of the already colorful neighborhood of Lapa. More than 60 different countries have contributed over 2,000 colored tiles to make this landmark what it is. Snapping a photo is all but mandatory. See page 65.

Visiting Cristo Redentor (Christ the Redeemer). Arriving at this New Wonder of the World (it was christened in 2007) is an arduous task thanks to the two million visitors who make the trek up Mount Corcovado every year. However, hours spent in lines amid selfiestick-wielding crowds hardly reaches Christ-like levels of suffering, and the 360-degree views of Rio afforded at the base of statue are enough to make anyone feel spiritual. See page 35.

Lazing on the beaches of the Zona Sur. Get that enviable *carioca* bronze whiling away the hours on Copacabana and Ipanema, two of the most iconic stretches of sand in the world. See pages 66 and 72.

Having a *chope* (draft beer) at Bar do Gomez. The secret's out – Bar do Gomez, located in Santa Teresa, is one of the best neighborhood bars in the world. The black-and-white photos on the walls are a historic record of the previous generations who ran this slice of 'Old Rio'. See page 113.

Browsing the handicraft stalls at Ipanema's Sunday 'hippie market'. You don't have to actually be a hippie to enjoy this Ipanema staple, which takes place every Sunday in the Praça General Osório. Arts and crafts abound, and shoppers on a budget can find great scores on souvenirs, gifts and bric-a-brac. See page 73.

Sampling exotic produce at a Feira Livre. Many of the fruits and vegetables on offer at these outdoor markets will be familiar. However, travelers likely won't know how to pronounce, let alone identify, some of the more exotic fruits, such as *guaraná*, *açai* and *graviola*. Pretty much everything can be made into delicious juices (see page 19).

Partying like a local at the Feira de São Cristóvão. Gigantic open-air market by day, raucous party venue at night – this is where to go for an authentic *carioca* party experience. Located a little outside the center, but well worth the taxi fare. See page 82.

Strolling through the Jardim Botânico. This delightfully fragrant enclave on Rua Jardim Botânico, the busy avenue that connects the Leblon and Botafogo districts, occupies 149 hectares (368 acres) and contains more than 7,000 species of tropical plants and trees and at least 140 species of birds. See page 38.

Attending Carnival. Behind-the-scenes activities of this most famous of festivals begin in November. Excitement spreads to every neighborhood and the powder keg of passion finally ignites during the last five days before Lent, when everybody joins the round-the-clock spree. With its frenzy of *bateria* (percussion), limber-legged dancing, singing, and resplendent costumes and bodies, Rio's annual extravaganza is one of life's overwhelming experiences. See page 23.

towering four-star hotels and luxury apartment buildings. But for all that, regardless of economic status, everyone from Rio has earned the moniker 'carioca'.

And what does it mean to be a *carioca*? Ask a hundred locals and you'll likely get 100 variations of the same answer: having a zest for life. If you ask people outside Rio (say, in São Paolo, for example), they'll probably tell you it means spending more time at the beach than at work. And *cariocas* are proud of this stereotype. Rio's people eat life in big bites, spending their time dancing, swimming, play-

---

TOP TIPS FOR EXPLORING RIO

Advance booking. For the winter and fall months it's possible to get away without booking too far in advance. However, during Rio's summer (Dec–Feb) it's best to plan ahead, and Carnival and New Year's Eve are unforgiving to those who arrive without a reservation. Book as far in advance as possible.

Tipping. It's customary to tip 10 percent in restaurants, although many eateries both large and small include this service charge in the bill. Taxi drivers don't expect tips, but rounding up the change to make it an even fare is common.

Getting around. Because petty criminals often work the bus routes, it's recommended to take taxis when traveling throughout the city. That said, those arriving at the international airport will want to consider taking one of the blue *frescão* buses into town, as it is a much cheaper alternative. Also, they have air-conditioning, reclining seats and Wi-Fi.

Tickets. For tickets to the top samba school parades (which for visitors will range from about $150 to more than

$1,000) you should check with travel agents and tour operators in your home country as they are able to reserve space through authorized Brazilian ground agents. Trying to purchase a ticket in Rio on arrival can be considerably more difficult and often more expensive. Even at the last minute, however, your hotel concierge should be able to score you a ticket – but at a price.

Restaurant reservations. Want a table at that exclusive restaurant in Copacabana Palace? That's going to require a reservation (which usually can be done online). However, any restaurant boasting fewer than four stars should be relaxed enough to accommodate walk-ins.

How to spend one weekend in Rio. On Friday, visit the Sugarloaf and then head to the Zona Sur for a stroll along the Forte de Copacabana. Spend Saturday lazing at Posto 8 in Ipanema beach and shopping in the city, then head to Santa Teresa for dinner and party 'til dawn at Lapa. Sunday brave the crowds at Christ the Redeemer and then stuff yourself at a *rodízio churrascaria* for dinner.

Ipanema beach

ing sports and whiling away the hours with close friends and family over a few beers and great food. Their over-riding ethos is that of inclusion, and *cariocas* welcome everyone with open arms – even tourists.

LOCAL CUSTOMS

Some knowledge of Portuguese is no doubt a useful things, but it's also important to also read the signs; *cariocas* are big on body language and hand signals. After just a couple of days, you'll find yourself giving the thumbs-up, just as they do, to com-municate 'OK' or 'thank you'. How-ever, if you touch your forefinger to your thumb – as in the American hand-gesture for 'A-OK' – you'll basi-cally be telling people where they can stick it. Other than that, *cariocas*, like most Brazilians, are very welcom-ing to foreigners, so there isn't much guesswork concerning how to navi-gate local customs.

POLITICS AND ECONOMICS

Brazil has seen many political mile-stones since the last dictatorship ended in 1985. Most notably these came in the form of populist and Workers' Party founding member Luiz Inácio 'Lula' da Silva being elected President in 2002, followed by his for-mer protégé, Dilma Rousseff, being elected in 2011. However, the lus-ter of Brazil electing its first female president has been lost in the subse-quent years as the administration has been rocked by a number of scandals, including the Petrobras oil scandal, in which state-run energy firm Petrobras was accused of inflating government contracts and giving kickbacks to the Workers' Party. This, combined with Brazil's recession and currency deval-uation in 2015, means public confi-dence in the government is at record lows. The country's economic insta-bility, when combined with its political uncertainty, makes it difficult to pre-dict what's in store for Latin America's largest economy not only in the long run, but in the near future as well.

Despite political turmoil and glaring poverty, and faced with an economic downturn and an uncertain future, Rio continues on an upward trajec-tory. Brazil played host to the World Cup in 2014 and the Olympic Games in 2016. Carnival will come again, and once more this sub-tropical paradise will be the focus of the entire world. It will attract everyone from jetsetters and aristocrats to street sweepers and paupers, all united in the spirit of music, dance and revelry. Because to be *cariocas* is to take life as it comes, accept it, celebrate it, and abandon all pretense and formality in the process. And just like the *cariocas*, the only thing you really need to enjoy Rio is a clear azure sky and an open schedule.

Acarajé (bean fritters)

FOOD AND DRINK

Rio's food scene is rich and varied. It's a great place to visit for epicureans who like a Michelin star with their meal as well as for gastronomic adventurers on the hunt for exotic and soulful flavors.

In the melting pot of Brazil, three different influences have intermingled deliciously to create the concept of a 'typical meal'. The Indians contributed vegetables, grains and an appreciation of seafood; the Portuguese, their stews and their sweet tooth; and the African slaves added new spices and sauces.

Rio was long São Paulo's poorer cousin in terms of dining options, but since the 1980s its array of international cuisines – French, German, Spanish, Portuguese and Italian, as well as food from more exotic locales – has improved significantly. Sushi, for example, is now ubiquitous here, and there are countless sit-down Japanese restaurants, delivery options, and *temakerias*. The most authentic *carioca* eating experiences, however, are based on four items: meat, served in *churrascarias* (barbecue houses), often *rodízio*-style (all you can eat); *feijoada*, the national dish; fish and seafood; and tropical fruits and vegetables. Other indispensable parts of the *carioca* diet are spicy foods imported from northeastern Brazil, notably Bahia.

The tourist zone, Zona Sul, contains the majority of the city's best restaurants. Also worth exploring at lunchtime is the central business district, which has a distinguished range of restaurants. Some of Rio's finest and most elegant dining is to be found in the restaurants of the top hotels in Copacabana and Ipanema, most notably the Copacabana Palace (Cipriani and Mee), Fasano (Fasano El Mare) and Sofitel Rio (Le Pré Catelan).

One craze is for restaurants at which you pay by weight. Called *Por Kilo* (or *A Quilo*), they range from *churrascarias* to Lebanese restaurants; many offer a bit of everything, and they are often the best bet for vegetarians and vegans since there is always an abundance of salad, rice and beans on offer. At between R$15 and R$25 per kilo of food, they represent tremendous value, and in many the quality is considerably higher than your average cafeteria.

BRAZILIAN CUISINE

Brazil's national dish is *feijoada*, and it's real *carioca* food. Dating back to the 19th century, this staple has been passed down through generations by moms and grandmas, all of them lovingly slow-cooking the dish over hours and even days. While most *cariocas* typically

Feijoada   *Street food*

eat it for lunch on weekends, in some places *feijoada* is served on Wednesdays. It's a feast of black beans with smoked sausage, pork products (tongue, tail, ear, etc.) and dried beef, flavored with onions, garlic, chives, tomatoes, parsley and hot peppers, then served with boiled rice, shredded kale and fried manioc flour, and finished with fresh orange slices to help with digestion. To taste home-cooked *feijoada* is to experience Brazil's version of 'soul food', such is this dish's depth and richness of flavors. It's humble food, rooted in poverty and even slavery, and a testament to what culinary heights people can reach when limited to the most inexpensive, common ingredients. Start the meal with a *batida* or *caipirinha* aperitif, and be ready for naptime once the experience is over.

From Brazil's southernmost state of Rio Grande do Sul comes *churrasco*, which is gaucho-style barbecued meat. *Cariocas* and tourists alike enjoy dining at *churrascarias*, where beef, sausages, chicken and chops are skewered and roasted over charcoal. Cuts to look for include *picanha* (rump steak), *fraldinha* (bottom sirloin) and *ponta de agulha* (short ribs). At all-you-can-eat *rodízios* the waiters arrive with one skewer after another, tempting you with a sausage, then a chop, then a steak, and so on, until you wave the white flag of surrender. You don't have to know the language, but you certainly need a big appetite.

Many Rio restaurants deal primarily in fish and seafood. Look for *zarzuela de mariscos*, a thick Spanish version of a bouillabaisse, or the Portuguese variants, *caldeirada* or *frutos do mar ensopados*. *Moquequas* (of fish, shrimp or crab) are a style of Bahian fish stew prepared in a covered clay pot. When they eat fish, *cariocas* generally prefer a thick fillet, so in many restaurants you'll find dishes described vaguely as *filet de peixe* (fish fillet). The fish in question often turns out to be *badejo* (bass), tasty in spite of its anonymity, but sometimes overwhelmed by a thick tomato sauce. You can also get excellent *linguado* (sole). The sauce called *belle meunière* is a butter sauce complicated or complimented, depending on your point of view, by the addition of shrimp, mushrooms, asparagus, capers and whatever else will make it seem luxurious. In Portuguese restaurants, you can choose from many varieties of *bacalhau* (dried salt cod), usually baked in a rich sauce.

Nibbling by the Water

Beach snacks are a staple of Rio's fast food scene. Regardless of which stretch of sand you're at, vendors will inevitably pass by offering everything from oysters and shrimp to cashews and popsicles. One of Brazil's most iconic (and delicious) beach nibbles is *queijo*, a skewer of hard white cheese roasted over open coals until charred and gooey. Always get it dipped in oregano and drizzled with honey.

Lunchtime at a restaurant in Lapa

'HURRY-UP' FOOD

Stand-up snack bars, known as *lan-chonetes*, are everywhere. They serve *lanches* – meaning snacks, not lunches, which is what you might guess. These are the places to try Brazilian appetizers, such as codfish balls, Lebanese *kibe*, shrimp pies or *pão de queijo* (cheese bread). Homemade Bahian treats like *acarajé* (bean fritter) and *vatapá* (shrimp stew) are sold on the streets.

A TASTE OF THE NORTHEAST

In the cuisine of northeastern Brazil, Indian, African and European currents meet. Rio has several good restaurants specializing in these spicy delights, which include:

Acarajé. A large fritter made from a batter of ground beans, deep-fried in boiling *dendê* oil, the yellowish palm oil indispensable to Bahian cooking. The resulting dumpling is split down the middle and liberally filled with *vatapá*, dried shrimp and hot *malagueta* pepper sauce. It is served as a starter or snack. Be careful; it can be wickedly hot.

Vatapá. This calls to mind shrimp creole, but it's more complicated, with subtly interacting flavors. The ingredients may include shrimp, fish, grated coconut, ground peanuts, cashew nuts, tomatoes, onions, hot peppers, ginger, coriander, olive oil, *dendê* oil, pepper and salt. This is thickened with breadcrumbs and served with rice cooked in coconut milk.

Xinxim (pronounced '*shing-shing*'). What differentiates this Bahian chicken stew from all other chicken-in-the-pot recipes is the addition of ground, dried shrimp and the use of hot spices and *dendê* oil. Approach the hot sauce served on the side with caution!

DRINKS

Cuba has the mojito; Brazil has the *caipirinha*. Both cocktails enjoy massive popularity because each mixes a few ingredients in perfect harmony. In the case of the *caipirinha*, the liquor in question is *cachaça*, which is distilled from sugar cane. Ice and lemon (or a sweeter cousin, *limão de Persia*) soften the blow of this potent concoction. Locals say the quickest way to ruin the drink is by using subpar alcohol, so always go top shelf at the bars. Also, limes should be cut to order, like the pros do at Academia de Cachaca, in Leblon (see page 115). The finished result always tastes best in a plastic cup lounging on the beach. Some locals do consider the *caipirinha* a 'tourist's drink', but don't take that at face value – it's not uncommon to see *cariocas* cooling off with this refreshing workhorse of a cocktail.

A *batida* is a cocktail – usually whipped up in a blender – of *cachaça*, ice, sugar and fruit juice.

Given the generally tropical temperatures, Brazilians don't drink a lot of wine, but that should not stop you from enjoying the excellent local wines, plus those

Bottles of cachaça

Fruit stall in Ipanema

from neigboring Chile and Argentina. *Cariocas* in general stick to Brazilian beer, a great national asset – always served very cold. Draft beer (*chope*) is the favorite, but some restaurants only serve bottled beer, usually in large bottles. Look for harder-to-find bottled beers such as Bohemia and Cerpa. If you can't get them, an Antártica or Brahma *bem geladinha* (well chilled) will do just fine.

Coffee, usually espresso-like *cafezinho*, is strong. Brazilians like their coffee very sweet, and very often.

SUCOS (JUICES) AND OTHER THIRST QUENCHERS

In the tropical heat, you'll work up a healthy thirst. But no matter where you find yourself, relief is close at hand. On the beach, barefoot salesmen shuffle past you every other minute offering soft drinks, mineral water, beer or paper cups filled with iced lemonade or *mate* (pronounced *mah-chee*) from their over-the-shoulder tanks. Here the *mate* is served very cold and sweetened; it tastes like tea with overtones of tobacco. Another typically Brazilian drink, bottled and swaggering with caffeine, is *guaraná*; it's made from a fruit from the Amazon forest and tastes a bit like cream soda. A great thirst-quencher is *água de coco*, or coconut water (it's a natural rehydrant).

Above all, though, look for the bars overflowing with fresh fruit. They serve *sucos* (juices), sometimes as many as 30 or 40 different fruits, some of them

exotic fruits you've never seen or heard of, squeezed as you watch. Don't limit yourself to the delicious orange juice; try some tropical specialties like *cajú* (cashew-apple), *mamão* (papaya), *maracujá* (passion fruit) or *manga* (mango). More exotic still are fruits from the north and northeast, including *graviola*, *cupuaçú*, *tamarindo* and the fashionable fruit of the moment, *açai*, dark purple and with a distinctive, strong taste. This blended wonder-berry is traditionally served at breakfast, often topped with banana slices and berries.

VEGETARIANS

Rio isn't exactly a hotbed for eateries catering to the herbivore lifestyle; there's no real vegan scene as of yet in the city, although one vegan restaurant, Vegetariano Social Clube in Leblon, is enjoying some success. Having said that, local cuisine invariably involves non-meat dishes like black beans, rice and salads. And the abundance of fresh fruits in the city (and indeed all of Brazil) means vegetarians won't ever have to search far for a snack or vitamin-packed *suco*.

Food and Drink Prices

Throughout this book, price guide for a two-course meal with a drink:

$$$$ = above $50
$$$ = $30–50
$$ = $15–30
$ = below $15

Fashion boutique in Ipanema

SHOPPING

Rio's shopping options cater to all tastes and income brackets. The modern shopping centers located in the Zona Sul are great mid-range options, while the chic wares found in Ipanema's boutiques are a must-visit for fashionistas.

Rio is a hot-zone of consumerism, and those with a charge card will find themselves as sated as they would be in Beverly Hills, Paris or Milan. The difference is that in Rio, designer labels can often be had for a fraction of the price charged in those other cities. Conversely, travelers on a budget can browse many of the local *feiras* for authentic clothing, jewelry, handicrafts and musical instruments, most of which can be had for a song.

WHAT TO BUY

Some of the items you may wish to take home from Rio include: art – particularly naïve and primitive works; antiques, from the shops along Rua do Lavradio or the antiques fair; *figas*, the Afro-Brazilian good-luck symbol in the form of a fist (to bring good luck, it must be given as a gift); handmade hammocks; jacaranda-wood salad bowls and trays; cloth kites in fighting-bird shapes and bright colors; leather bags, belts, wallets and shoes; musical instruments, such as the *berimbau*; recordings of samba, bossa nova and MPB (*música popular brasileira*); and

swimsuits (if they're not too risqué for the beaches you frequent back home). Brazil is also a leader in world fashion and currently many of even the most fashionable boutiques offer excellent value when compared with Europe and North America.

Precious gemstones are sold in such varied places as hotels, downtown stores and even on city streets. The most popular buys are amethysts, aquamarines, opals, topaz and tourmalines, but diamonds, emeralds, rubies and sapphires are also mined in Brazil. Check with your consulate concerning customs regulations if you are considering a purchase.

MAIN SHOPPING AREAS

Ipanema

Ipanema is home to the most sophisticated boutiques in the city. The main shopping drag is Rua Visconde de Pirajá, but it is well worth exploring the side streets and the new shops that always seem to be popping up. Those who need to pick up a sarong, bikini, or pair of sunglasses can head to any of the beach vendors, and visiting the

The Saara bazaar area in Centro

Sunday 'Hippie Fair', located at Praca General Osório (9am–6pm), is a must. Here visitors can find arts and crafts including paintings, leatherwork, carvings, tapestries and many other items.

For gems and precious stones, head to the west side of Ipanema. The two best-known and most reputable dealers of gemstones, H. Stern and Amsterdam Sauer, have branches in this area, and they also offer free museum/workshop tours. H. Stern's headquarters is at Rua Visconde de Pirajá, 490 (tel: 21-2106 0000; www.hstern.net); Amsterdam Sauer's is at Avenida Garcia D'Ávila, 105 (tel: 21-2512 1132; www.amster-damsauer.com).

Copacabana and Botafogo

Copacabana has more options for shoppers than Ipanema (except where it concerns clothing) and prices are generally lower. It's a great area to go for casual-wear and beachwear. Most *cariocas* do their shopping at the big malls such as Shopping RioSul (Rua Lauro Müller, 116; www.riosul.com.br), located in Botafogo just before the tunnel leading into Copacabana. Famed swimwear retailer BumBum (www.bumbum.com.br) has a location here, and no, thongs are not the only option.

Soccer fans can get their jerseys in Copacabana at Loja Fla (Avenida N.S. de Copacabana, 219; www.lojafla.com.br). They are well stocked in every piece of Flamengo apparel and products you can imagine. Be forewarned, wearing a local jersey, like those of Flamengo or Botafogo, means you are adding your voice to the chorus of millions of rabid *futbol* fans. Expect heated but good-natured competition. Also, Loja Fla can personalize any jersey by printing the customer's name on the back.

Northern zone

To arrive in the north, take any bus marked São Cristóvão or grab a cab. Feirarte II (Thu–Fri 8am–6pm), at the Praça XV de Novembro, offers dolls, jewelry, embroidery, leather goods and musical instruments (and Bahian food).

SALES

The best places to score deals on goods are generally at the aforementioned *feiras* and open-air street markets. For retail sales, head to any of the city's shopping malls.

OPENING TIMES

Shops and stores are generally open 9am–6pm, but in certain neighborhoods they have much longer hours, sometimes opening before 8am and closing around 10pm. Shopping centers, like Rio Sul and BarraShopping, open 10am–10pm, except on Sunday when Rio Sul opens at noon and BarraShopping at 1pm. Some businesses close for lunch between noon and 2pm. Some local food stores open Sunday morning.

Celebrating on the streets

ENTERTAINMENT

Come for the beaches, stay for the music. And the dancing. And the parties. And the festivals. The 'ands' could go on forever, because if it's one thing cariocas are proud of, it's that they live in one of the most entertaining cities in the world.

Any place that boasts being the home of the 'world's biggest party' probably isn't lacking for things to do. And this is certainly true of Rio de Janeiro. The city is an international entertainment destination, where folks flock to get away from the mundane and the familiar and revel in the exotic and exciting. Those who've never danced before might just be tempted to bust out an impromptu *sambinha* (little samba) on the dance floor, and folks without rhythm could wind up on a street corner banging away on a *tamborim* amid a group of local amateur musicians. Day or night, there's always entertainment to be had in Rio.

DANCE AND MUSIC

Dance and music are the predominant expressions in Rio de Janeiro (as well as in Brazil in general), and the two go hand in hand. Simply put: everyone dances in this city. The most popular dance is the samba (referred to as the 'Brazilian Waltz' in some circles), and it has many variations, all defined by their exuberance, sensuality, and quick steps on the quarter beat. It's such a part of the city's character that thousands of people practice for months for one purpose: to put on the grandest display of dance and music in the world come Carnival time. But you won't just see people moving during festivals. The local *cariocas* tend to tap out a tune on a simple matchbox or tabletop, even as they sip a cold beer, and dancing is sure to break out sooner or later. Going to a show with the locals is a special treat; for an unusual but authentically *carioca* night out, try a *gafieira* (dance hall), where locals go to shake up the dance floor (see page 114).

Rio is home to countless Brazilian musicians and composers who cover every Brazilian musical form from MPB (*música popular brasileira*) to *frevo*, and *choro* to *forró*. Brazil has a vast spectrum of musical talent, but some of the big names to look out for are Adriana Calcanhoto, Ana Carolina, Bebel Gilberto, Caetano Veloso, Carlinhos Brown, Chico Buarque, Daniela Mercury, Gilberto Gil, Ivete Sangalo, João Gilberto, Jorge Benjor,

Dancer at the Sambódrome   *Carnival costume*

Maria Bethania, Maria Rita, Marisa Monte, Milton Nascimento, Ney Matogrosso, Paralamas do Sucesso, Titãs, Vanessa da Mata and Zeca Pagodinho, to name just a few.

Among the many great Brazilian composers and performers who continue to shine from beyond the grave are Antonio Carlos Jobim and Elis Regina and, from the world of classical music, Heitor Villa-Lobos.

CARNIVAL

Carnival. No other party in the world can touch it. In fact, Rio's legendary annual outburst of music, color and *alegria* (joy) is probably more dazzling than you could ever imagine. Even Hollywood, with the biggest budget in history, could never come close to producing such an authentic outpouring of emotion and energy.

Although a breathtaking spectacle, at its most basic Carnival is an expression of popular culture. More than half a million people – all in costumes they may have paid a large chunk of their annual salary for – march, dance and sing their hearts out in the organized samba school (see page 114) parades. Thousands more revel, in and out of fancy dress, at parties and informal secondary parades. High society and many tourists, including foreigners, join the frenzy in exclusive and fashionable masquerade balls. Whether neighborhood children with makeshift snare drums or a band of polished musicians perform the music, though, samba during Carnival is contagious.

In Rio, the last fling before the austere Lenten season starts in earnest the Friday before Shrove Tuesday (Mardi Gras). It goes on for five days and five nights – more than 100 hours of almost non-stop revelry.

NEW YEAR

The New Year's celebrations in Rio, known as Reveillon, are almost as big an attraction as Carnival itself. Based on and around Copacabana Beach, they are one of the most spectacular ways of seeing in the New Year anywhere in the world. On 31 December, over three million people, the vast majority dressed from head to toe in white, make their way down to the beach at Copacabana. As well as being New Year's Eve, it is also the feast of Iemanjá, goddess of the sea, and elaborate altars are built in her honor placed as offerings in the sea.

Just about every apartment along the beach, and certainly all the hotels, host parties and the focal point to kick off the celebrations is a huge fireworks display at midnight that covers the whole of Copacabana. The party carries on through the night with live music on stages all along the beach. Many hotels start serving special breakfasts from 5am onwards.

View of Botafogo Bay in 1880

HISTORY: KEY DATES

From kings and slaves to dictatorships and democracy, Rio de Janeiro has experienced much since it was first colonized as a tropical backwater. The 1900s saw Rio's rapid transformation into the internationally renowned metropolis it is today.

RISE OF THE NEW WORLD

1494	Treaty of Tordesillas divides the New World between Spain and Portugal; Portugal receives territory that will become Brazil.
1500	Pedro Álvares Cabral is the first European to set foot in Brazil, which he names Ilha de Vera Cruz.
1502	Portuguese explorers encounter Guanabara Bay on the 1st January, naming it Rio de Janeiro (January River).
1555	The French build a garrison on the site of present-day Rio de Janeiro.
1567	Governor general Mem de Sá expels the French; Rio de Janeiro is founded.
1695	Discovery of gold in Minas Gerais leads to the growth of gold-rush towns in the interior.

FROM VICEROYS TO THE REPUBLIC

1763	Capital transferred from Salvador da Bahia to Rio de Janeiro.
1808	King João VI flees Portugal to escape Napoleon and establishes his court in Rio.
1821	João returns to Portugal and names his son, Pedro, as prince regent and governor of Brazil.
1822	Pedro I proclaims independence from Portugal and establishes the Brazilian Empire, which is recognized by the US and, in 1825, by Portugal.
1831	Pedro I abdicates in favor of his five-year-old son (later Pedro II).
1889	Pedro II is overthrown by the military and sent into exile; the republic is declared.
1930	Getúlio Vargas takes power after a revolution.
1931	Statue of Christ the Redeemer is inaugurated.

Brazil fans on Copacabana beach during the 2014 World Cup

GROWING PAINS

1937	Vargas creates Estado Nôvo, a populist dictatorship.
1950	Brazil hosts the fourth World Cup, the first after World War II. Matches take place in six cities, including Rio. Vargas again made president, this time in a democratic election.
1954	On the brink of military coup, Vargas commits suicide in the presidential palace.
1960	Capital transferred from Rio de Janeiro to Brasília.
1964	Military coup overthrows president João Goulart.
1967	A new constitution is drawn up; General Artur da Costa e Silva is inaugurated as president.
1968	A military coup closes Congress and gives Costa e Silva dictatorial powers; another, revised constitution is promulgated.
1974	Economic miracle fails; foreign debt soars.

MOVING FORWARD

1979	João Baptista Figueiredo becomes military president. Amnesty issued to all who had been persecuted by military.
1985	Military regime steps down; democracy is restored. Rock in Rio, Brazil's largest rock festival takes place, with an estimated 1.5 million attendees.
1989	Fernando Collor de Melo elected in direct presidential elections.
1992	Rio de Janeiro hosts Rio 92 (United Nations Conference on Environment and Development).
1994	Real Plan (and new currency) introduced to tame inflation.
2002	Populist Luiz Inácio Lula da Silva ('Lula') becomes Brazil's first left-wing president for 40 years.
2007	Rio hosts the Pan American Games. The Christ the Redeemer statue is voted one of the New Seven Wonders of the World in a global poll.
2011	Dilma Rousseff, a former protégé of Lula da Silva, becomes Brazil's first female president.
2014	Brazil hosts the FIFA World Cup. Matches are held at venues in 12 cities, including Rio's Maracanã stadium.
2016	Rio hosts the 2016 Olympic and Paralympic games.

BEST ROUTES

1. Sugarloaf and Praia Vermelha   28
2. Corcovado and
      Christ the Redeemer   33
3. Botanic Gardens   38
4. Santa Teresa   44
5. Botafogo   49
6. The Centro: Rio's Downtown   55
7. Cinelândia and Lapa   61
8. Copacabana   66
9. Ipanema and Lagoa   72
10. Zona Norte   78
11. Niterói   83
12. Paquetá Island and
      Guanabara Bay   89

Sugarloaf cable car

SUGARLOAF AND PRAIA VERMELHA

Enjoy a thrilling ride on the cable car to the summit of Sugarloaf Mountain, with panoramic views of Rio. A leisurely stroll takes you back down to tiny Praia Vermelha Beach and through tropical forest along the coastal Claudio Coutinho Trail.

> **DISTANCE:** 4km (2.5 miles)
> **TIME:** Minimum 3 hours
> **START/END:** Sugarloaf ticket office
> **POINTS TO NOTE:** To avoid the long lines for the Sugarloaf cable car during the peak season and at weekends, arrive before 9.30am or after 3.30pm. Come on clear days for the best views and towards the end of the day to see the sunset and the lights come on in Rio. The entire route, except for some small sections, is wheelchair accessible.

Along with Corcovado, the Sugarloaf is Rio's most famous mountain. Instantly recognizable by its shape, it was supposedly named for its resemblance to the cones of pressed sugar exported to Europe in colonial days. Coincidentally, the early inhabitants of the Rio area, the Tamoio Indians, called the mountain *Pau-nh-açuquā*, which means 'high, pointed mountain standing alone'.

The Sugarloaf is 396 meters (1,299ft) high and it rises dramatically straight out of the sea, at the entrance to Guanabara Bay. Its vertical slopes are composed of bare granite, estimated to be 600 million years old. In the same complex, Morro da Urca is the lower and broader hill. Between the two is a shoulder of dense tropical forest.

Since 1912, cable cars have been taking tourists to the top of Sugarloaf. Spectacular views and the thrill of the ride make this one of Rio's top attractions.

UP THE SUGARLOAF BY CABLE CAR

The **ticket office** ❶ and start of the cable car journey up the Sugarloaf is by the tiny **Praia Vermelha Beach** in the **Urca neighborhood** (Avenida Pasteur 520; tel: 21-2546 8400). Most people come by taxi, but it's also served by bus No. 511 from Ipanema and No. 511 107 from the Centro (Downtown) and Flamengo. Alternatively, a 10-minute walk away is the Rio Sul shopping mall, a major stop for buses connecting Copacabana and Ipanema to Botafogo and the Centro.

The view from the Sugarloaf   *Gazing down on Rio*

Tickets cost R$71 for adults; half price (on presentation of ID) for 6–21 year-olds, over 60s and disabled visitors; free for children under 6 years. Tickets can also be bought online (www.bondinho.com.br/site/en), but exact dates must be chosen. Opening hours are 8am to 7.50pm and there are trips up every 20 minutes (or when the cable car fills up). Each leg of the cable car journey takes 3 minutes.

Morro da Urca

The first cable car ascends 220 meters (722ft) to **Morro da Urca** ❷. Stand on the right for a view over the little beach, Praia Vermelha. As you exit, on show on your left are the first two generations of cable cars. As you walk round, there are views straight down to Botafogo Bay, a sheltered spot with bobbing yachts, and along the Niemeyer-designed tropical gardens of the Flamengo waterfront. The skyscrapers of the Centro appear behind the runway of Santos Dumont airport. Striding across the bay is the 13km (8-mile) -long bridge linking Rio to Niterói, the city on the other side. Britain's Queen Elizabeth II attended the ceremony marking the start of construction work on it in 1968, and the bridge was officially opened to traffic six years later.

Benches under trees make this a relaxing place to admire the view. At this level, there are cafés, souvenir shops and the **Cota 200 Restaurante** ❶. There's also an amphitheater which stages parties and music events (especially in the summer between New Year and Carnival) and the **Cocoruto**, a high-tech museum focused on the history of the cable cars. At this first level, you can also book short helicopter flights along Copacabana Beach.

Sugarloaf Summit

If you thought the first cable car was thrilling, wait until the second to the **Sugarloaf Mountain** ❸. It soars over the forest below and then

Taking a break on Morro da Urca

momentarily hovers at the top of the Sugarloaf's vertical granite walls, before coming into dock.

There are several pathways and seating areas around the summit, allowing you to take in views of different parts of the city, as you walk around. There are also plenty of cafés and souvenir shops up here. Looking back towards Morro da Urca from where the cable car ascended, Botafogo neighborhood is squeezed between hills, with the Christ the Redeemer statue, atop Corcovado, towering above it. Along the coast, to the left, you see the long stretch of Copacabana Beach, with the flat-topped peak of Pedra da Gávea in the distance. In the other direction, the whole of Guanabara Bay unfolds, with the hills and beaches of Niterói on the far side. On clear days, you can make out the 2,275-meter (7,464ft) -high Serra dos Orgãos Mountains, the highest range which rise up behind the Bay. Thin rock pinnacles on the right include the Dedo de Deus ('God's Finger').

Towards the back of the summit, on the seaward side, there are steep paths heading down into an area of forest, with marmosets and picnic tables. Not many people make their way here, so it's a good place if you want to get away from the crowds and enjoy some peace and quiet, and perhaps a picnic too.

When you eventually retrace your steps and make landfall back at sea level, Rio's layout and its chaotic beauty will make much more sense to you.

GENERAL TIBÚRCIO SQUARE

Exiting at the base of Sugarloaf, head across the road to the landscaped central square, the **Praça General Tibúrcio ❹**. It's named in honor of a Brazilian General who fought in the 1864–70 War of the Triple Alliance. This pitted Brazil, Argentina and Uruguay against Paraguay. Casualties were high on all sides, but it decimated Paraguay, which is estimated to have lost around 70 percent of its adult male population. In the center of the square, the 15-meter (49ft) -high Monument to the Heroes of Laguna and Dourados depicts a retreat of part of the Brazilian troops from Paraguay, many suffering from cholera.

On the far side of the square is a complex of tall buildings, all belonging to the Brazilian military. You'll realize that many of the most beautiful spots on Rio's coastline are military areas: a legacy of Portuguese colonial rulers defending the city against other European powers.

PRAIA VERMELHA

On the seaward side of the square is a small sandy stretch wedged in between two massive granite mountains: the Sugarloaf on the left and Morro de Babilônia on the right. **Praia Vermelha ❺**, meaning Red Beach, isn't as red as one would imagine, but it does have some earthy ocher tones. The setting is certainly dramatic and the view out to sea features the hills of Niterói up the coast. It's a popular weekend and sum-

A quiet day on Praia Vermelha

mer hangout, but if swimming, beware of strong undertows. The water can be clean, but more often than not is polluted by the outflow from dirty Guanabara Bay, just around the corner.

The promenade, with benches under tall palm trees, is a pleasant place to rest. Often, there are carts here selling fresh popcorn and tapioca, a type of crêpe originally from northern Brazil. It's made with cassava flour and usually comes with a choice of sweet or savory fillings.

At either end of the beach are remnants of the **Praia Vermelha Fort**. Founded in 1701, it once spanned the entire length of the beach, but it was destroyed in 1935 during a failed uprising against Getúlio Vargas, the dictatorial President of Brazil (who ruled from 1930–45 and 1951–4). The old battlements on the right now house **Terra Brasilis** ❼, a bar and restaurant with live music. The left side is now home to the Gabriela Mistral Infants School, named after a revered Chilean poet and teacher, awarded the Nobel Prize for Literature in 1945.

PISTA CLAUDIO COUTINHO

To the left of the school is the entrance to the **Pista Claudio Coutinho** ❻, a 1.25km (0.75-mile) walk, open daily from 6am to 6pm. This is one of Rio's lesser-known treasures and it's preserved from the intrusions of modern life by the prohibition of bicycles, cars, motorcycles and skates; the natural wildlife is kept safe by the no-pets policy.

A paved pathway hugs the mountainside. To your right, the sea beats against the barnacle-covered rocks. To your left, the forest is punctuated by bare granite rocks with prehistoric-looking bromeliads. Early on in the walk, you will come across a grotto, to your left, dedicated to **Our Lady of the Conception**, patron saint of the Brazilian military. Notice how the ferns sprout enthusiastically from the rocky

Rock Climbing on the Sugarloaf

As unlikely as it sounds, the first (recorded) person to reach the summit of the Sugarloaf was a British nanny. Upon reaching the summit on a solo attempt in 1817, Henrietta Carstairs duly planted Britain's flag, the Union Jack, into the peak. It was removed the following day by a Portuguese officer from the army at the base of the Sugarloaf, who presumably was the second person up there.

Nowadays, the Sugarloaf and the adjacent Morro de Babilônia, both with bare granite surfaces, are among the most popular rock climbing spots in Brazil, with over 60 routes. Walking around the base of the Sugarloaf or going up it, keep an eye out for these adventurous souls. If interested, there are professional guides who take small groups up to the top, and there are options from beginners to advanced levels. If you do get to the top, the journey back down on the cable car is free.

Terra Brasilis, Praia Vermelha

altar. Look back to your right for a view of Praia Vermelha.

Hummingbirds dart in and out of the light in dive-bombing movements that are hard to catch on film but wonderful to see. Gentle, hissing squeaks from the trees indicate the presence of another form of life: marmosets, always playfully curious, popping their white-tufted ears out of their tree homes to check out the pass-

ing human traffic. Weighing a mere 8.5oz (240g), these little creatures hate the cold so they are in their element here, and, provided they can avoid joining the food chain via the ever-watchful birds of prey, they can live for up to 20 years.

At all times of the year, the vegetation on the walk is breathtaking: black-eyed susans, giant elephant-ear philodendrons, blue gingers and pinky-purple epidendrum orchids. Brazilwood trees have been planted on the seaside of the walk; these slow-growing giants will one day create an impressive avenue. Fruit trees do well here, too, including mango, papaya and avocado. The birds know this and are present in great number and variety. The yellow waistcoats of the great kiskadees are everywhere and even if you cannot see them, you can hear their rackety calls. Pairs of powder-blue sayaca tanagers dance gracefully through the trees. The real prize, though, is the blood-red Brazilian tanager.

The walk ends rather abruptly at a lookout. Across the small bay in front of you is Cotunduba Island and hilltop Leme Fort. Beyond the lookout, there is a dangerous trail leading up the rocks. In fact, all along the walk are the starting points of hikes of varying degrees of difficulty, including a main one about half way along that takes you up to the first level of the cable car, Morro da Urca. It's recommended that you do these with a proper guide. All that remains now is to retrace your steps, enjoying the walk all over again as you do so.

Food and Drink

① COTA 200 RESTAURANTE

Morro da Urca (Sugarloaf), Avenida Pasteur 520; tel: 21-2543 8200; www.cota200 restaurante.com.br/en/; Mon–Sun L and happy hours, Wed–Sun D. $$$
Contemporary Brazilian, French and Italian cuisine, in a modern glass structure.
The best part is the panoramic view of Botafogo Bay and Corcovado Mountain. In the evenings, drinks and small bites are served as the lights of Rio twinkle below.

② TERRA BRASILIS

Praça General Tibúrcio, Praia Vermelha; tel: 21-2275 4651; www.restaurante terrabrasilis.com.br; daily L and D. $$
Set within the old battlements of a former fort, this spot is right above Praia Vermelha Beach, with the Sugarloaf Mountain as a backdrop. It has an outdoor bar terrace and live Brazilian music in the evenings. Brazilian seafood dishes and barbecued meats, along with pizzas and fondues, are the specialties.

View of Corcovado from the bay

CORCOVADO AND CHRIST THE REDEEMER

This half-day tour takes you to the Christ the Redeemer statue, one of the world's greatest landmarks, traveling by cog train through the rainforest. After taking the spectacular views, come down to earth and visit an endearing museum of naïve art.

DISTANCE: 1.6km (1 mile) of walking, plus the train ride
TIME: Half a day
START: Estação do Trem do Corcovado, Cosme Velho
END: Largo do Boticário, Cosme Velho
POINTS TO NOTE: If going by taxi, make it clear that you want the 'Estação do Trem do Corcovado' on Rua Cosme Yelho. Otherwise the driver may take you all the way to the top of the mountain, which you do not want. You can stay at the top for as long as you like and board any train to come back down. Services at the top are basic, but there's a decent café/restaurant and clean toilets. There are restaurants available at the end of the trip, on Rua Cosme Velho.

The official name of Rio's most stunning monument is Cristo Redentor (Christ the Redeemer), and the 710-meter (2,329ft) -high mountain upon which it is perched is called Corcovado, which translates as 'hunchback'. Cristo Redentor has been here since 1931, when it was hauled up in pieces on the train. Made of reinforced concrete clad in soapstone, the monument was made in France under the supervision of Paul Landowski. Its dimensions are staggering: 30 meters (98ft) high, sitting on an 8-meter (26ft) -high pedestal. The distance between the statue's fingertips is 30 meters (98ft), and the entire monument weighs 1,145 tons. It faces the mouth of Guanabara Bay and can be seen from many parts of Rio (when other mountain peaks and skyscrapers are not in the way).

THE CORCOVADO COG TRAIN

Although there is a road up to Cristo Redentor, a more charming journey is on the little red cog train, with its large windows and old wooden seats. It's been in operation since 1884, when Emperor Dom Pedro II first made the trip.

The Corcovado Train Station

The journey departs from the no-less picturesque train station, the **Estação do Trem do Corcovado ❶** (Rua Cosme Velho

Conductor on board the train to Corcovado

513; tel: 21-2558 1329; www.corcovado. com.br; daily 8am–7pm; R$62 for adults in high season, with discounts for children and over-60s; free for children under the age of 5 if sitting on a lap; tickets at the entrance, online and at several ticket offices in town; see website for details). Trains depart every half-hour, and the trip takes some 20 minutes; 345 passengers an hour can be transported, and there is generally a fast-moving line at the ticket counter. They normally only sell as many tickets as there are seats, so you don't have to worry about missing the train, or not getting a seat. There's also a small café at the station. If, on an exceptionally busy day, your ticket is for the next-but-one train, pop along to the Museu Internacional de Arte Naïf (see page 36) to fill the time.

Try for a seat on the platform side, on the right as you look up to the statue, as there is a good photo opportunity as you approach the top. That said, when the train is full there is such a scramble for cameras and window space that few people actually get to record the shot they want. The seats are sheer wood, and quite slippery. Be prepared to knock knees with the person opposite, as space is tight.

Floresta da Tijuca

As the train leaves the station, it passes tantalizingly close to some run-down but

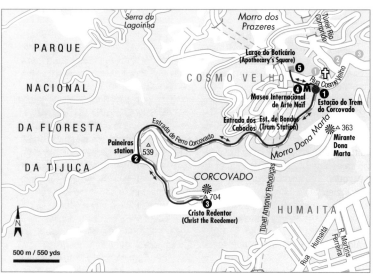

Trem do Corcovado   *Christ the Redeemer statue*

attractive buildings before entering the **Floresta da Tijuca** (Tijuca Rainforest), the largest urban forest in the world. Much of the original forest was cleared in the middle of the 19th century and given over to coffee plantations. These did not prosper but left wide-open, unprotected tracts of land, provoking soil erosion and destroying the habitats of numerous animals, as well as affecting the city's water supply. Things reached such a state that the emperor undertook a pioneering environmental project in the area, the replanting of the Tijuca Rainforest. This was started in 1881, under the supervision of a certain Major Archer, who, with the help of half a dozen slaves, planted some 100,000 trees over a 13-year period. The result is a lush, damp, fern-filled forest floor below, and a canopy of rich green above.

The train travels at a mere 15kph (9.5mph) on the way up, so you can really get a feel for the variety of vegetation. Mosses and ferns cling to the permanently damp rocks and you'll notice how much cooler it is under the canopy than in the city. The enormous golden fruit of the *jaca* trees (similar to breadfruit) hang patiently from the barks of the trees until it is time to splatter to the ground. The brightly colored faces of busy lizzies (*Impatiens*) are everywhere, and it may come as no surprise to know that they are called 'Shameless Marys' in Portuguese.

Along the route, there are occasional sections where the forest cover clears, allowing for panoramic views over Rio.

Near the top, an ultra-steep section passes close to a drop-off with a glimpse of the Lagoa Rodrigo de Freitas lagoon. The only stop en route is at the **Paineiras station ❷**, where you sit for a few minutes, waiting for the down train to pass. Built in 1880, Paineiras has been many things in its time, including a private residence and a hotel. It had its moment of glory in the 1970s, when the victorious Brazilian national soccer squad was based here. It is due to reopen as a visitor's center and ticket office in 2016.

The Cristo Redentor Monument

When you get to the top of the Corcovado, there is an unruly, excited rush to disembark and see the **Cristo Redentor ❸**. Let the crowds go ahead of you and take it easy – there is nothing to hurry for. It is often windy up here and skirts will swirl, as will swarms of dead wasps that have flown too close to the spotlights. The statue itself is impressive, but you are almost too close to appreciate the detail and magnitude of it. At the base of the statue is a tiny chapel, dedicated to Nossa Senhora Aparecida, the patron of Brazil. It is seriously at odds with the grandiosity all around it and not what one would expect from this exceptional religious site. The altar is tackily decorated with artificial flowers and the floor littered with coins, thrown as offerings by the faithful.

Views of Rio

The views cannot be described, only experienced. From this height you can appre-

View from Corcovado

ciate just what an enormous city Rio is, and how tightly it is squeezed between the mountains and the sea. You also realize that you, as a visitor, will not see it all, especially the industrial zones and the favelas towards and beyond the airport. You can see that the Rodrigo de Freitas lagoon is very large indeed, and that Ipanema occupies a crowded, narrow band of land. You can measure how much prime real estate the Jockey Club occupies, and how green the Jardim Botânico is. In the other direction, you can recognize how ambitious an undertaking the construction of the Rio-Niterói Bridge was, and what a difference it has made to the city. The flying saucer shape of Maracanã soccer stadium sticks out a mile, as do the vast expanses of densely occupied land, often overhung by a pall of polluted air.

Make your way slowly around, using the maps on the railings to get your bearings. These are especially useful if there is a sudden change in the weather and you are cloaked in mist. If this should happen, and it frequently does, just be patient band wait a while, as the clouds rush past and views should be revealed in no time at all. There's a café up here too, which has tables on a terrace with a panoramic view.

MUSEU INTERNACIONAL DE ARTE NAIF (MIAN)

Once you've come back down the mountain, as leave the train station, turn left for the **Museu Internacional de Arte Naïf** ❹ (International Museum of Naïve Art; Rua do Cosme Velho 561; www.museu naif.com; Tue–Fri 10am–6pm, Sat–Sun 10am–5pm; minimal admission charge). This historic house has around 6,000 paintings in a museum overflowing with vibrant color. Children will enjoy the paintings and the museum has been set up in a child-friendly way.

The term naïve is applied, generally speaking, to art as practiced by the self-taught, free from the influences of formal artistic trends or schools. Brazil takes its place with France, the former Yugoslavia, Haiti and Italy among the world's top five exponents of the style. Here, in this intimate little museum, you will see the best Brazil has to offer. As you walk in, you are immediately hit by the impact of a vast canvas, measuring 4 x 7 meters (13 x 23ft), by Lia Mittarakis, entitled *Rio de Janeiro, I Like you, I Like your Happy People*, a quotation from one of the city's favorite old-time waltzes.

Wander around to capture the lack of inhibition, the undisciplined use of color and the sheer cheek of the works on display. Another quotation catches the eye, this one by Einstein: 'Imagination is more important than knowledge', a judgement that perfectly sums up the concept of naïve art. One unmissable work is Aparecida Azedo's *Five Centuries of Brazil*. Viewed from a mezzanine level, it measures a staggering 1.4 x 24 meters (4.5 x 78.5ft). Key events in Brazilian development are shown with bold simplicity,

Largo do Boticário

and explanations of the historical scenes depicted are given on the railings of the mezzanine. Before leaving the museum, make the most of the glassed-in shop, which has high-quality, artistic items on sale. Excellent reproductions of Brazilian art, as well as some originals, make easy-to-pack mementos of your day. If a trip up Corcovado gave you a feel for the city's geography, then MIAN will have provided a perfect glimpse into its history, culture and pervading mood.

APOTHECARY'S SQUARE

As you leave the MIAN, turn left again and a little way up the hill on the other side, at Rua Cosme Velho 815, you come to the Beco do Boticário, a narrow street at the end of which is the **Largo do Boticário** ❺ (Apothecary's Square). This appealing little piece of old Rio, set among shady old trees, was put together in the 1920s in neocolonial style with materials taken from demolition sites in the center of the city. What it lacks in authenticity it more than makes up for in charm. The houses are privately owned, and therefore cannot be visited, but the square is a perfect stop for a photo opportunity and a few moments of quiet contemplation.

RUA COSME VELHO

By this stage, you may be wanting something proper to eat and drink. If you're not in a hurry to catch a taxi back to your hotel, there are several options within walking distance, all on Rua Cosme Velho. **Luna Café** ❶ is the closest option, just across the road from the Museum of Naïve Art. Following Rua Cosme Velho downhill you'll see **Assis** ❷ after about 300 meters/yds, then **Mamma Rosa** ❸ after 600 meters/yds.

Food and Drink

❶ LUNA CAFÉ
Rua Cosme Velho, 564; tel: 21-3264 4678; www.lunacafe.com.br; Tue–Sun L and D. $
This is a quick and easy option with a Brazilian buffet (paid by the kilo) and menu. Decor is simple and outside there are garden terraces.

❷ ASSIS
Rua Cosme Velho, 174; tel: 21-2205 3598; www.lunacafe.com.br; daily B, L and D. $
Named after the writer Machado de Assis, this cozy café and bookshop is situated in his former home. Sandwiches and lunches are served at little tables.

❸ MAMMA ROSA
Rua das Laranjeiras, 506; tel: 21-2556 6502; www.mammarosa.com.br; daily L and D. $$
Hearty Italian pastas and pizzas are served in a traditional trattoria setting, decorated with checked tablecloths.

BOTANIC GARDENS

Stroll around Rio's Jardim Botânico, a tropical Garden of Eden with majestic palms, immense trees from the Amazon, orchids and colorful birds. Cool clear streams flow through the grounds and there's even a section of native rainforest. Museum spaces, cafés and restaurants enhance this relaxing itinerary.

DISTANCE: 3.2km (2 miles)
TIME: 3 hours
START/END: Jardim Botânico front entrance
POINTS TO NOTE: This is a perfect spot for those seeking a cool and shady place in the heat of the summer and although it gets busier at weekends, it never feels too crowded. The entire route is wheelchair accessible and there are also guided tours of the grounds on motorized buggies. There is a café near the entrance, plus another one once inside the gardens.

The Botanic Gardens were born of a king's desire for a decent cup of tea, improbable though that may sound. Established in 1808 by Dom Joao VI – as were so many things in the city – the garden was intended as a nursery where exotic imports such as tea and spices could be tested and eventually acclimatized to the local conditions. In contrast to current bans on the importation of plants, in those days the practice was encouraged

and tax incentives were made available to those who wanted to bring new plants into the country. Since the early 19th century, the garden has grown to become one of the most important centers for botanical research in the world, as well as the city's favorite recreation area, visited by thousands of people each year.

You will encounter brilliantly colored heliconia plants and crazy cannon ball trees, also known as monkey's apricots. Look at the tops of the trees for some interesting surprises: bromeliads in the canopy provide perfect bathtubs for birds. You have to be quick to snap the darting hummingbirds with your camera, and extremely lucky to capture the toucans. Human biodiversity is also present: joggers, meditators, lovers and bridal parties – the Botanic Gardens are a favorite spot for wedding photographs.

JARDIM BOTÂNICO

For this itinerary, take a taxi to the **vehicle entrance ❶**, not the old twin-tower pedestrian entrance in the middle of the palm avenue. If catching a bus, and there

Avenue of royal palm trees at the Jardim Botânico

are plenty to Gávea, the closest stop is outside the Jockey Club (ask for Joquei). The Jardim Botânico (Botanical Gardens; tel: 21-3874 1808/3874 1214; www.jbrj. gov.br; Tue–Sun 8am–5pm, Mon noon–5pm) is at Rua Jardim Botânico 1008.

Over 6,000 plant species thrive on its 189 hectares (467 acres), which are also home to more than 120 species of birds. Apart from the tour highlighted here, there are guided tours on electric buggies. Maps with additional information, and suggested trails, are also available at the entrance.

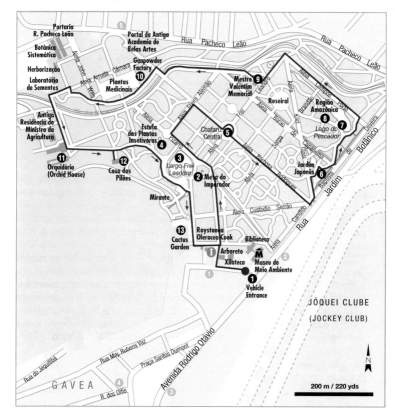

Bamboo grove

Museu do Meio Ambiente

Immediately on your right, as you enter the gates, is an classic-style manor house painted white. This is the **Museu do Meio Ambiente** (Environmental Museum; Mon noon–5pm, Tue–Sun 9am–5pm; free). Inaugurated in 2008 to commemorate the bicentenary of the Botanic Gardens, it houses small art exhibits and hosts environmental programs. Although small, it's worth having a look inside.

Espaço Tom Jobim

The main path takes you to a series of little building clustered around a pond, about 100 meters/yds further on. Once used as workshops and warehouses, these have been converted into a cultural center, with a theater and spaces for art exhibits. Named in honor of Tom Jobim, Rio's renowned bossa nova musician (who composed 'The Girl from Ipanema' in the 1960s), this area is free to enter. One of the houses is taken up by **La Bicyclette** ①, a high-end French-style café (once inside the Botanic Gardens, there is a simpler outdoors café). On the other side of the pond, by the entrance into the gardens, you'll see the ticket office and a souvenir shop (with a good selection of botanical books).

Once you're through the turnstiles, turn right (unless you need to use the bathroom to your left). You'll notice that the pathways (called *aleias*) have signposts on most corners. Use these to follow this route. You'll also find the information plaques interesting.

Head to the right on Aleia João Gomes, and then take a left on to Aleia Warming, named after a Danish botanist who was active in Brazil in the 1860s. On your right are massive mango trees blocking out the sunlight. Cross over Aleia Custodio Serrão, and soon you will reach a small hillock topped by a stone summer house, the **Mesa do Imperador** ② (Emperor's Table). Here the royal family enjoyed their picnics at a giant stone table, with a view of the Corcovado Mountain. The lake lying before you, **Lago Frei Leandro** ③ has giant *Vitoria regias* lily pads.

Carnivorous Plants and Bamboo

Continue down Aleia Pizzaro, leaving the lake behind you to your left, and get to know the carnivorous plants housed in a greenhouse just ahead of you in the **Estufa de Plantas Insetívoras** ④. Turn right onto Aleia Freire Alemão, shaded by dense bamboo. Russian composer Nikolai Rimsky-Korsakov was especially impressed by these bamboos when he saw them on his round-the-world naval cruise in 1862. Look out for the darting movements of the spotted rail, called a water chicken *(frango d'agua)* in Portuguese. To your left are massive *jatobá* trees, whose hard pods when bashed open yield a dry yellow substance, which is edible and particularly good if crumbled into milk.

Imperial Palm Avenue

The next (main) right turn takes you along the Aleia Barbosa Rodrigues, lined with

The English–made Chafariz Central

the imperial palms which are the hallmark of the garden. Straight ahead is the impressive central fountain, the **Chafariz Central ❺** made in England, paying homage to music, art, science and poetry. To the left of the fountain is a majestic *sumaúma* tree, with jutting buttress roots. Known as a kapok or silk-cotton tree in English, it can reach a height of 70 meters (230ft) and produces a fluffy fiber which was traditionally used as a stuffing for life jackets and teddy bears.

Japanese Gardens

Keep heading down Aleia Barbosa Rodrigues to the iron gate between two towers on the busy Jardim Botânico road. Here, turn left onto Aleia Karl Glass. Suddenly and unexpectedly the fertile opulence of the tropics is replaced by the precision and calm of the Orient. The **Jardim Japonês ❻** is an exotic microcosm, complete with a lotus pond and sculpted granite blocks whose plinths are mondo grass, native to Japan and Korea. Crossing over the little bridge and Aleia Barão de Capanema, you are back in Brazil with a jolt, smack in the middle of the rainforest. A typical, thatched Amazon dwelling perches on the lakeside, the **Lago do Pescador ❼**, with a sculpted fisherman.

Amazon Region

Continue ahead, with the lake on your left, until you reach Aleia Campos Porto, also signposted as the **Região Amazônica ❽**, or Amazon Region. Walk left along a stunning avenue of giant Amazonian trees, the

pau mulattos or *mulateiros*, which completely shed their bark every year. When new, the bark is like polished bronze, ending up dun colored when it is ready to be shed.

The Amazonian Indians have multiple uses for this readily available material: topically, it is used to treat wounds, while a concentrated tisane taken regularly is used to cure diabetes. Other tribes anoint themselves with a decoction of the bark: as it dries on their skin it forms a barrier against parasites and fungal infections.

Mestre Valentim Memorial

When you reach the end of the Aléia Campos Porto, there is an attractive pond guarded by sculptures of Echo and Narcissus. Tum left onto Aleia Frei Leandro and admire the line of spindly clove trees along the way. In summer, tiny pink cloves cover the ground, ready for collecting and drying. The cool, peaceful summer house on your right, with angels' trumpets on gate duty, is the **Mestre Valentim Memorial ❾** in honor of the 19th-century sculptor responsible for most of the statuary in the garden. Turn right onto Aleia Barão de Capanema, bordered by young mango trees. Follow the Rio dos Macacos (Monkey River), where you might see egrets wading, any number of rufous bellied thrushes and occasionally toucans.

The Old Gunpowder Factory

Take a right when you hit Aleia Barbosa Rodrigues and cross over the river;

The Orchid House

turn left again, and follow the river. After stands of banana and cocoa trees, to your right are the ruins of the **Gunpowder Factory** ⑩, also established by João VI, which blew up in 1831; only the bare walls and the gate remain. Within, there are swings for the children, restrooms and a casual outdoors café. The other half is taken up the **Medicinal Garden**, with the entrance around the corner on the right.

Bromeliad and Orchid houses

Upon leaving the old Gunpowder Factory, continue straight on, with the Macacos River on your left. To your right are the offices of the **Research Institute**. Cross over a steep little planked bridge. Over the other side on your right is a stand of *pitanga* trees, which grow at the back of beaches and produce a bittersweet fruit, also known as a Brazilian cherry. In front is the **Bromeliad House**, where you will see what a multiplicity of interesting relatives the domestic pineapple has.

Out into the daylight again, turn right, passing the mustard-colored administration building on your right. Observe the old man's beard, or Spanish moss, cloaking the trees. Next is the **Orchid House** ⑪, with species clearly labeled, but not necessarily in flower.

Casa dos Pilões

Straight ahead, as you exit, is Aleia Alberto Lofgren, with the archeological display in the **Casa dos Pilões** ⑫, guarded by huge millstones and shaded by Malay apple (*jambeiro*) trees. In season, they drop

needle-like, shocking-pink petals, which form a carpet. Coming back out, head immediately right, up a slope. This is the Aléia Caminhoá, which takes you into the wildest section, the Atlantic Rainforest (Mata Atlântica). As you walk along, you'll get a feel for Rio's original vegetation and meet the giants of the Brazilian tree world, the iron wood tree, noble mahogany and the brazilwood tree that gave the country its name.

If you want to explore this area more, there are various pathways off to your right, heading further up the hill and into the forest. Sticking to the main path, you'll pass a lookout house on your right and cross a tumbling stream as you near the entrance again.

Cactus and Sensorial Gardens

Up to your right is the large **Cactus Garden** ⑬, where plants from arid regions contrast with everything you've seen so far. Around the corner is the tiny **Sensorial Garden**. Designed with the visually-impaired in mind and with signs in braille, the garden is planted at waist height, with a clever mix of scented and textured plants.

Finally, as you reach Aleia João Gomes, near the start of the walk, look up into the canopy of the large tree in the corner and you may see the round pods of the Brazilnut. Behind this is an imperial palm, *Palma Filia*, offspring of the first imperial palm brought here from Mauritius, which was planted by Dom João VI in 1809.

The Cactus Garden

JARDIM BOTÂNICO RESTAURANTS

By this stage, you may be ready for lunch, dinner or a drink. If you go back to the entrance you'll be on busy Rua Jardim Botânico again. Straight ahead of you, across the other side of the road is the Jockey Club and about 100 meters/yds to the left is the high-end **Rubaiyat** ❷ steakhouse. Alternatively, if you walk 400 meters/yds to the right, you'll find a couple of other steakhouses at the Jockey Club entrance, including **Prado** ❸. Another 200 meters/yds will get you to the casual cafés and restaurants around Praça Santos Dumont in Gávea (you may want to take a taxi), including **Hipódromo** ❹. If you head left out of the Botanic Gardens entrance, walk (or taxi) 500 meters/yds to the end of the gardens until you reach the first road, Rua Pachecho Leão. Head left up this to a series of bars, cafés and *bistrôs* in charming village-like Horto, including **Bar do Horto** ❺.

Food and Drink

❶ LA BICYCLETTE
Rua Jardim Botânico, 1008; tel: 21-3594 2589; www.labicyclette.com.br; Tue–Sun Br and L. $$
Apart from the tropical vegetation of the surrounding Botanic Gardens, it feels as if you're in a trendy café in France, enjoying croissants, baguette sandwiches and tarts.

❷ RUBAIYAT RIO
Rua Jardim Botânico, 971; tel: 21-3204 9999; www.rubaiyat.com.br/rio; Mon–Sat L and D, Sun D. $$$
This high-end *churrascaria* serves succulent steaks and premium wines in a sophisticated yet relaxed setting. Thu–Mon you may see horses thunder past on the racecourse below. Reservations recommended.

❸ PRADO
Praça Santos Dumont (main entrance to the Jockey Club); tel: 21-2512 2247; daily L and D. $$
As you eat your steak, pizza or gourmet burger, enjoy the view through large glass windows of thoroughbred horses warming up before the weekend races.

❹ HIPÓDROMO
Praça Santos Dumont, 4, Gávea; tel: 21-2274 2755; daily B, L and D. $$
A traditional *carioca choperia*, with simple decoration and a relaxed vibe, serving cold beers, bar food and steaks in a dining room open to the street.

❺ BAR DO HORTO
Rua Pacheco Leão 780, Jardim Botânico; tel: 21-3114 8439; Tue–Sun L and D. $$
Situated inside a renovated manor house and decorated with craftwork, this bohemian little spot offers classic Brazilian dishes, mouth-watering *caipirinhas* and live music in the evenings.

Arcos da Lapa

SANTA TERESA

Visit one of Rio's most picturesque and bohemian neighborhoods, Santa Teresa, by taking a tram from Downtown Rio, across the Arcos da Lapa and up the hillside. Here, you'll be able to enjoy views over Rio, take in historic architecture and find a charismatic little place for a drink or meal.

DISTANCE: 1.6km (1 mile) walking, plus the tram ride
TIME: A half day
START: Estacão do Bonde, Centro (Downtown Rio)
END: Largo de Guimarães (Santa Teresa)
POINTS TO NOTE: The tram station (open 7am–9.30pm) can get busy with tour groups, especially between 10am and 4pm in the peak Summer season. The Chácara do Céu, a highlight of this visit, only opens at noon and is closed on Tuesdays. The Parque das Ruinas is closed on Mondays. There are plenty of bars and restaurants, some with live music in the evenings, especially at weekends.

THE SANTA TERESA TRAM

Getting to Santa Teresa is half the fun, so make sure you go on the tram, or *bonde*, as it's called. You start from the **Estacão do Bonde** ❶ (Rua Lélio Gama, next to the Petrobras building in the Centro; trams start at 7am and end at 9.30pm). It's a 5-minute walk from **Carioca** or **Cinelândia** metro stations, but if coming by taxi be firm with the driver (so that he doesn't take you up to Santa Teresa instead). The station seems like a little bit of garden in the bustle of the business core of Rio, where the buildings tower above you. Tickets for the tram are ludicrously cheap, and the simple, old-fashioned vehicle seems to have been left over from days gone by. All aboard, and amid much shouting and carrying-on by the driver and conductor, off you trundle. Quaint it may be, but quiet it isn't. Hang on tight; it isn't hard to imagine bouncing right out of the tram. Velcro on your behind, or rodeo experience, would not go amiss here.

The tram clanks its way over the magnificent **Arcos da Lapa** ❷, the disused aqueduct that strides over the Lapa region. Vertigo sufferers should try not to look down. Before long, you are clanking up toward

Santa Teresa tram   *Street art in Santa Teresa*

Santa Teresa. The views are magnificent, a different take on the familiar contours made famous through postcard images of the city. Notice how, in this land of natural plenty, vegetation springs from every patch, and even from the roof tiles themselves.

PARQUE DAS RUINAS

Tell the tram driver you are going to the *museu* (pronounced moo-zeu) and he will drop you off at the **Largo do Curvelo ❸** which is signposted and the first proper 'station' with a mini 'platform' in the middle of the road. As you disembark, you'll see to your left a viewpoint over Guanabara Bay. On the other side of the road from this, there is a raised pathway alongside a wall, which you follow to **Parque das Ruinas ❹** (Ruins Park; Rua Murtinho Nobre 169; tel: 21-2215 0621/2224 3922; Tue–Sun; 8am–8pm; free), a 5-minute walk away. This is the former home of society hostess Laurinda Santos Lobo, whose parties, held on the fourth day of every month,

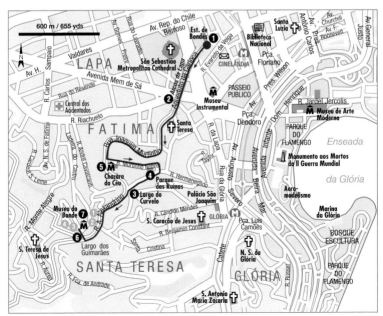

A busy street corner in Santa Teresa

attracted the likes of dancer Isadora Duncan and writer Anatole France, as well as the cream of Rio society. On her death in 1946, the building was abandoned, and fell into disrepair. By 1995 it was truly a wreck, and architects Emani Freire and Sonia Lopes rose to the challenge of restoring it, without, as they put it, 'frightening the ghosts away'. They seem to have succeeded, for the place has an extraordinary feel to it, combining ancient with modern, crumbling bricks with tubular steel. Cross the giant sundial in the courtyard floor. There's also an art exhibition space, an outdoors theater and a viewpoint with a 360-degree view of Guanabara Bay and the Sugarloaf.

CHÁCARA DO CÉU

Your next stop is the **Chácara do Céu** ❺ (Little Villa in Heaven; Rua Murtinho Nobre 93; tel: 21-2224 8981; http:// museuscastromaya.com.br; daily except Tue; noon–5pm; free on Wed). It is right next door to the Parque das Ruinas, although you have to go round the corner to reach the entrance. This is the former residence of Raymundo Castro Maya (1894–1968), a stylish industrialist, entrepreneur and art collector, who also gave wonderful parties. Most of the house is laid out as a museum, and provides a personal view of life at the top in the middle of the last century. It is fitting that the home of this man, who loved Rio

and did so much for the city, should be open to visits by all.

There are treasures all around, not least of which is the solid wooden staircase, made of peroba wood, now on the endangered-species list. The house was built in 1954 and was considered fiercely modern for its times. The effect of natural daylight can be experienced in every room and the integration of the house with its surrounding garden is complete. Works by Picasso, Dalí, Matisse and Miró are dotted around the walls.

While the collection is no rival for major international museums, it is still thrilling to see works by artists such as these hanging on the walls of what is, in effect, a private home. The Dufy in the library is a gem; it shows a French beach, complete with tricolor flapping in the wind, and the beach-goers are

Santa Teresa botequim

Colonial buildings in Santa Teresa

all decked out in shirts and ties and long dresses – a far cry from Ipanema. Castro Maya's two passions, Rio and art, have resulted in one of the most important collections of Brazilian art to be found anywhere. Works by Guinard, Ibere Camargo and the now very collectable Di Cavalcanti are all on display, and the Chácara also houses many works by Candido Portinari (1903–62), possibly Brazil's best-known artist. There are also watercolors and drawings by Jean Baptiste Debret (1768–1848), a French artist whose work brought to life the Brazil of the early 19th century.

For the foreign visitor, the 'Brasiliana' collection, including pictures of Rio, hold special appeal, as you can see the familiar outlines of the mountains uncluttered by development. You can experience this in the stunning Thomas Ender oil painting (1848) at the top of the stairs.

The garden is a magical spot, also with 360-degree views of Rio. The city is so close that you feel you can touch it, but far enough away that it is silent. The garden is home to numerous birds, and also to some evil-looking but harmless lizards. The mango tree dominates the lawn, and the flamboyant tree splashes its flame-colored summer blossom against the austerely modern lines of the house.

Allow yourself time to return to the front door, at the bottom of the stairs, because the little shop has some tasteful souvenirs. There is a sister museum, the Museu do Açude, in the Floresta da Tijuca (Tijuca Forest, Estrada do Açude 764, Alto da Boa Vista; Wed–Mon 11am–5pm; free on Thu).

LARGO DOS GUIMARÃES

Follow your footsteps back to the Largo do Curvelo tram stop. If there's a tram heading left up the hill on **Rua Almirante Alexandrino**, you may wish to hop on it, otherwise, it's a 5-minute walk with views of Downtown Rio to your right. As you go along, you'll start to pass a collection of bars and restaurants, also on your right, including **Adega do Pimenta** ❶ and **Bar do Arnaudo** ❷ plus old-fashioned general stores, selling just about everything from buckets and candles to bags of rice and beers, the sort of shops where they still polish the oranges before piling them high in neat pyramids. There are also plenty of craft shops – Santa Teresa has always been an arty place – so this might be the time to stock upon gifts or mementos to take back home with you.

You'll soon reach **Largo dos Guimarães** ❻, a point where several roads meet. You'll see more restaurants and gift shops here. Off to the right, there are signs to the two-roomed **Museu do Bonde** ❼ (Rua Carlos Brant 14; daily 9am–4.30pm; free) in an old tram garage down a cobbled street. A humble little spot, it's worth a stop if

Adega do Pimenta

you're interested in trams or railways – the memorabilia here harks back to the days when trolleys were pulled by mules – or want to see some excellent photos of Rio in the olden days. Take a good look at the gate to see what interesting effects can be created with bits of twisted wire and steel.

It is probably time for something to eat or drink by now, so make your way back to the Largo dos Guimarães. Within a short walk, you've got a huge choice of cafés, bars and restaurants, generally all within historic buildings. Apart from the places you passed on the way, a couple of other recommendations, just off to your right are **Rústico Bar e Restaurante** ③ and **Bar do Mineiro** ④ on Rua Paschoal Carlos Magno. See Restaurants (page 112) for more dining options in Santa Teresa.

To head back down, either catch the tram into the Centro, the bus (some go to Largo do Machado and others to Lapa) or a taxi (although these can be infrequent) to Zona Sul.

Food and Drink

① ADEGA DO PIMENTA
Rua Almirante Alexandrino, 296, Santa Teresa; tel: 21-2224 7554; daily L and D. $$
This hole-in-the-wall is a slice of old Germany, where you'll find bratwurst sausages and sauerkraut. Wash them down with artisan ales in a rustic wood setting, crammed full of antique memorabilia.

② BAR DO ARNAUDO
Rua Almirante Alexandrino, 316, Santa Teresa; tel: 21-2146 6704; daily L and D. $$
This tiny, family-run restaurant, decorated with old *cachaça* bottles, serves authentic cooking from Northeast Brazil. Portions are large. Dishes include *aipim frito* (fried manioc), *cabrito ensopado* (goat stew), *carne de sol* (sundried beef), *farofa* (fried manioc flour) and *feijão* (black beans).

③ RÚSTICO BAR E RESTAURANTE
Rua Paschoal Carlos Magno, 121, Santa Teresa; tel: 21-3497 3579; www.cafecito. com.br; Thu–Tue L and D. $$
As the name suggests, this is a rustic spot, serving pint-sized beers, contemporary Brazilian dishes and pizza. From the street, you walk up many steps beside an old manor house, and once you get to the top, you'll find tables either indoors or dotted around a garden terrace, under shady trees.

④ BAR DO MINEIRO
Rua Paschoal Carlos Magno, 99, Santa Teresa; tel: 21-2221 9227; www.bardo mineiro.net; Tue–Sun L and D,. $$
This classic *botequim* lined with old wall tiles and memorabilia is very popular, so come early if you want to bag a table. Hearty servings of *feijoada* is the specialty as are the beers, which areusually drunk on the pavement.

View over Botafogo from the Santa Marta favela

BOTAFOGO

Get to know the streets of one of Rio's traditional neighborhoods, once the home of the city's elite. Between apartment blocks and tiny shops, you'll pass elegant manor houses. You'll also find museums related to a politician, a music composer and Brazil's Indian tribes. End with a trip on a funicular up through a favela.

DISTANCE: 5km (3 miles)
TIME: A half day
START: Botafogo Metro Station
END: Cobal do Humaitá
POINTS TO NOTE: If visiting Santa Marta favela at the end of this tour (or any favela in Rio), take a note of the precautions highlighted in the boxed article. Away from the sea breeze, it can get hot and sticky walking around the streets of Botafogo, but there are plenty of little cafés en-route to buy drinks. The end of this route ends up in a former market which has plenty of options for lunch, dinner or a drink.

Botafogo, a traditional middle-class neighborhood between the Sugar-loaf and Corcovado, is hemmed in by steep hillsides and filled with apartment blocks, manor houses and bohemian cafés. Between the hills, it forms a sort of funnel shape, with the narrow end at Humaitá, meeting Lagoa Rodrigo de Freitas and Jardim Botânico. The wide end opens out onto Botafogo Bay, with a little beach and a panoramic view of the Sugarloaf.

Back in the 18th and early 19th century, this was one of the wealthy parts of Rio and at that time it was on the outskirts of the built-up area (Copacabana and Ipamena were still undeveloped beaches). With plenty of space, Botafogo was home to wide avenues and elegant manor houses with landscaped gardens. You can still see these dotted around the neighborhood, and several have been turned into museums. You'll also see smaller houses, often with two stories and painted in bright colors. These were the homes of merchants and tradespeople, with shops on the ground floor opening onto the street. In the 20th century, tall apartment blocks were built and the wealthy moved out towards the Lagoa and the coast at Ipanema and Leblon.

Often overlooked by visitors, it's an interesting place to wander around if you're wanting to get a feel for an authentic, untouristy, neighborhood. There are interesting museums and architectural styles. Cafés and casual

Botafogo by night

restaurants are everywhere, along with a buzzing nightlife and a touch of the arts scene.

BOTAFOGO

Start the walk at **Botafogo Metro Station 1**. If arriving by metro itself, take exit (A) Rua São Clemente – Humaitá. Head straight out of the exit (with a row of modern bars and eateries on your left: you may want to come back later. Head up the busy Rua São Clemente, with even street numbers on your right. As you walk along, you'll notice a mixture of architectural styles. Small two-story houses from the early 1900s are painted in bright colors, and have shops in the ground floor opening out onto the street. In the early 20th century, these would've been the most common building style along Rua São Clemente, but now tall residential blocks dominate. Occasionally, you'll see graceful manor houses, like the one housing the Center of Architecture and Urbanism of Rio de Janeiro on your left after one block.

Look ahead and up and you'll see Christ the Redeemer atop Corcovado Mountain looming above Botafogo and

starting straight down the street at you. Notice how steep the mountain is on the left side.

THE RUI BARBOSA HOUSE-MUSEUM

After about 200 meters/yds you'll reach the **Museu Casa de Rui Barbosa 2** (Rui Barbosa House-Museum; Rua São Clemente 134; tel: 21-3289 4600/ 3289 4667; www.casaruibarbosa.gov. br; Tue–Fri 10am–5.30pm, Sat–Sun 2–6pm). You'll realise that the former owner of this grand 19th-century manor house must have been an important man. Rui Barbosa, who was born in the state of Bahia in 1849 lived here from 1895–1923. An intellectual figure,

he became an eminent lawyer, author, diplomat and politician, serving as Brazil's Finance Minister (1889–91) and Bahia's State Senator for many years (1890–1921). He unsuccessfully ran on four different occasions to become the President of Brazil.

The Garden

In the front garden, there's a tall frangipani, with fragrant white blossom in the Spring. Below this, the rounded bushes are camellias, which the Portuguese originally introduced to Europe from their 16th-century voyages of discovery to Japan. Eventually they reached Brazil, where in 1888 they were planted by supporters of the movement for the abolition of slavery.

If you walk around the left side of the house, you'll see the appropriately-named cannonball tree (also known as a monkey's apricot), which has large pink flowers in the spring, followed by heavy round seedpods attached to the trunk in the summer. Around the back of the house are old shady mango trees and wooden benches, a popular spot for Botafogo mothers and nannies with their babies. To the right are the old stables, which nowadays house three old horse-drawn carriages and one of the earliest motorised cars produced, a Benz from 1903.

The House

Inside, it's like a giant step back in time. After Rui Barbosa died in 1923, the house and its contents were bought by the Brazilian state, and it feels like nothing has changed since. In 1930 it became a house-museum, one of the first of its kind in Brazil. The house was built in 1850 and it has a classic feel to it, with hardwood flooring, but surprisingly modest bedrooms, bathrooms and kitchen. It seems that about half the house is taken up by Rui Barbosa's 37,000 books, all in glass cabinets. In the ballroom, 'Buenos Aires' piano room and the 'Pro-Allies' room, there are beautiful furnishings and small oil paintings.

THE VILLA-LOBOS MUSEUM

A short walk takes you another manor house and museum, that of the renowned Brazilian composer, Heitor Villa-Lobos (1887–1959). To get there, keep walking up Rua São Clemente, until you reach Rua Sorocaba, four streets up on your left. Walking down it, you'll notice trees with pale trunks, the *pau-ferro* (iron wood), named for being extremely hard. At No. 200 on your right, the manor house is the **Museu Villa-Lobos** ❸ (Rua Sorocaba, 200; tel: 21-2226 9818; www.museuvillalobos.org.br; Mon–Fri 10am–5.30pm; free).

Born in the neighborhood of Laranjeiras, on the other side of the Corcovado Mountain from Botafogo, Villa-Lobos is regarded as one of Brazil's, and South America's, great-

An exhibit at the Museu do Indio

Favela Pacification

The '*pacifacação das favelas*' was a process which began in earnest in 2008. In simple terms, its objectives are to reduce gun-related violence in the city, while at the same time provide basic public services to Rio's poorest communities. The first step usually involves heavily-armed military police entering a favela, often followed by a shoot-out against drug lords and their gang of armed supporters. The next step is to set up a police post (UPP; *unidade de polícia pacificadora*) which then tries to retain control over the favela. After this, the city authorities are able to come in and improve on the very basic infrastructure, with, for example, better roads, sanitation and schools. The area generally becomes more attractive to live in, favela tours start and hostels spring up.

Of course, it's not as perfect as it may seem. The favelas remain a dangerous place: shoot-outs still happen and the drug trade continues. However, it's much better than it was, and the favelas around the Zona Sul which have benefited the most (like Vidigal, Santa Marta and Babilônia), are a world away from what they were. If you want to visit a favela, go with a professional guide. Not only is it safer, you'll also learn more and contribute towards someone's livelihood. Be respectful towards residents and don't do anything which could end you up in trouble (like snapping away with your camera or exploring too deep through alleyways).

est classical musicians. He helped define a new style, Brazilian Modernism, which blended early 20th-century European music with uniquely Brazilian elements. As a child, he was taught classical music by his father, but, much to his parents despair, as a teenager he started hanging out in neighborhoods and streets where informal samba and *choro* music gatherings took place. These were incorporated into his music, as were the sounds of folk music from around Brazil. As he started to get noticed, he moved to Paris in the 1920s. Here, he and his wife hosted Sunday *feijoada* lunches to fellow musicians.

As he toured European capitals, he became an internationally-recognized composer. In his later years back in Rio, now the 1930s and '40s, and with the support of the then-President of Brazil, Getúlio Vargas, he focused on education. Classical music and singing projects were introduced into schools across the country, reaching the masses and poorer segments of the population. They were also a way of disseminating Brazilian national identity in a period when the world was unstable and Brazil was under military dictatorship.

The museum follows Villa-Lobos' life and preserves his musical collections and some of his personal belongings. Touchscreens enable you to listen to some of his most famous pieces.

Favela bathtub

THE INDIAN MUSEUM

Upon exiting the Villa-Lobos Museum, turn right and walk to the end of the street, where you meet another busy road, Voluntários da Pátria. If you're in need of a drink or snack, pop into **Catarina Doces e Salgados** ➊ on the corner. Then, take the first right onto Rua das Palmeiras (which might be missing a street sign). The Indian Museum, **Museu do Índio** ➍ is on your right about half way down the street (Rua das Palmeiras, 55; tel: 21-3214 8719; www.museudoindio. gov.br; Tue–Fri 9am–5.30pm; Sat– Sun 1–5pm; free). Set in the grounds of your third manor house in quick succession, this museum takes you on a journey into the world of Brazil's native Amerindians.

At any one time, there are several exhibitions on show, and these tend to stick around for several months. They explore different aspects of the life of the hundreds of tribal communities in Brazil, through displays, photos and videos. It's done in a multimedia sort of way, and should be of interest to most children. The main exhibit space is upstairs in the main house. In the gardens are smaller spaces, along with areas where events take place (check the website for upcoming ones). The little shop in a mud and thatch hut has an excellent collection of craftwork from different tribes, at reasonable prices.

THE SANTA MARTA FAVELA

Turn right and walk towards the end of Rua das Palmeiras. As you do so, look up on the hill ahead of you and you'll see colorful favela (shanty-town) houses. Many of these houses were painted for free, as a social project, by the Tintas Coral paint company. On the right side of it, you'll notice the tram lines of a funicular which heads straight up the hillside. At the end of Rua das Palmeiras, you'll rejoin busy Rua São Clemente, and across it, there's a little park with a playground, **Praça Corumbá** ➎.

Visiting the Santa Marta Favela

It's recommended to visit favelas with a guide (see page 52), but if you're interested and confident in visiting the Santa Marta favela on your own, cross over to the park and head up the road on its left side, Rua Barão de Macaúbas. The first 400 meters/yds of the road curves gently around and you'll notice brightly-painted walls and lots of little roadside stalls, each one selling something different, from barbecued meat skewers to bags of dried beans and bottles of shampoo. The road buzzes with residents from Santa Marta coming to and fro, and little bars with music add to the vibe. At this stage you're basically at the edge of the favela.

Carry on around the corner and when you see the favela proper rise up on a steep hill in front of you, look to your right, where the **Santa Marta funicu-**

Colorful facades in Santa Marta

lar ❻ starts. It's free to go up, but if you come around lunchtime or at the end of the school day you may have to wait 20 minutes or so. Waiting patiently in the line will be mothers and school children. The funicular is a simple glass cabin, which has several stops on its straight journey up the hill. For panoramic views, get off at the final stop, where you'll see the whole of Botafogo below you and the Corcovado up on your right. There are a couple of little bars up at the top. You can either catch the funicular back down, or walk down the steep steps (of which there are several routes). About half way down there is a statue to Michael Jackson on a rooftop viewpoint. It was here and in the city of Salvador that his song 'They Don't Care About Us' was filmed.

COBAL DO HUMAITÁ

From Praça Corumbá, either catch a taxi or walk along Rua São Clemente. After about 250 meters/yds, this road veers off to the left and as it does so it becomes the tree-lined Rua do Humaitá. Go another 250 meters/yds and on your left you'll reach the **Cobal do Humaitá** ❼.

This covered space, which takes up a whole city block, was once a market for fresh produce, flowers, meat, seafood and more. Part of this still exists, but nowadays it's also home to a large number of bars and casual restaurants. In the evenings and at weekends, the place buzzes with crowds of *cariocas* and live music. There's a wide selection, including pizza joints and sushi bars. For a cold beer on a table outside, try **Espírito do Chopp** ❷ or for Brazilian food (with a beer or *cachaça*) try **Joaquina** ❸.

Food and Drink

❶ CATARINA DOCES E SALGADOS

Rua Voluntários da Pátria, 236; tel: 21-2527 1531; www.catarinadocesesalgados.com.br; daily B, L and D. $

This little café is modern, clean and air-conditioned: a handy stop for a coffee or cold drink, with a good selection of savory pastries.

❷ ESPÍRITO DO CHOPP

Cobal do Humaitá; tel: 21-2266 5599; www.espiritodochopp.com.br; daily L and D. $

As the name suggests, the focus here is on *chopes* (draft beers) which are served on plastic tables and chairs outdoors. They also serve casual food, including steaks, soups and crêpes.

❸ JOAQUINA BAR E RESTAURANTE

Cobal do Humaitá; tel: 21-2527 1722; www.joaquina.com.br; daily L and D. $$

A wide range of *petiscos* (cod fritters and more), plus meat kebabs, pizzas and sandwiches are served with very cold beers in a casual setting.

Rua Uruguaina

THE CENTRO: RIO'S DOWNTOWN

Stroll through the Rio's historic heart, home to an imperial palace, a cluster of museums on cobbled streets and an ornate hilltop monastery. Then join the revitalized Guanabara Bay waterfront, with its ultra-modern museums and wide open spaces.

DISTANCE: 5km (3 miles)
TIME: A half day
START: Praça Quinze de Novembro (ferry terminal in the Centro)
END: Museu de Arte do Rio, Praça Mauá, Centro
POINTS TO NOTE: Many of the sights (including museums) are closed on Mondays. The CCBB Museum is closed on Tuesdays. During the week, the Centro is busy with office workers. Things quieten down at weekends, especially on Sundays when streets are practically empty. Beware of pickpockets in this area, and avoid walking around late at night. Along the way, there are numerous cafés, bars and restaurants.

The Centro, Rio's Downtown, is often overlooked by tourists (and *cariocas* alike) as a place to visit. Much more famous (and on everyone's list of must-sees) are the iconic Sugarloaf and Corcovado peaks, beaches like Ipanema and Copacabana, and, of course, Carnival and samba music.

A trip to the Centro is for those in search of culture. No other place in Rio can compete in terms of museums, architecture, churches and history. In the past, this is where Rio grew up and where the Portuguese royal family lived for a few years when they fled Napoleon's invasion of Portugal in 1808.

As Brazil's capital from 1763 to 1960 (when it moved to Brasilia), this was the political and commercial center of an immense country. So, as you walk around, you'll see reminders of the past in its historic buildings, including numerous churches and elegant European-style buildings. Sections remain of early 20th-century commercial streets, still narrow and cobbled. Traditional *botequims*, serving beers and lunches, on little outdoor tables, are everywhere. The city buzzes with workers and traffic.

As you approach the end of the route, you'll see the revitalized port area, transformed between 2014 and 2016. Here, there are wide open spaces with granite paving, views of Guanabara Bay and a couple of world-class museums focusing on art and science. It's a calm

Casa Cavé, Rua Sete de Setembro

way to end a journey through the heart of old Rio.

PAÇO IMPERIAL

Your starting point is the **Paço Imperial ❶**, the old Imperial Palace (Praça Quinze 48; Tue–Sun noon–7pm; free), which is easily reached by taxi, bus or a 10-minute walk from Carioca metro. A simple, symmetrical edifice, this building served as the first official residence of the Portuguese royal family – but not for very long, as they found the air too fetid and the surrounding streets too dirty for a longer stay. In its time the palace has served many purposes, among them that of central post office. Inside is a small historical museum and upstairs there are rooms for temporary art exhibits and performances. There's also a book and music store with a café, plus a casual bistro and the Atrium Restaurant (see page 106).

PRAÇA QUINZE

When you re-emerge into the square, **Praça Quinze de Novembro ❷**, take a few minutes to visit the waterfront, overlooking the Bay of Guanabara. This is the point of departure for ferries to Niterói and Paquetá. Two equestrian statues dominate the square; one commemorates the victories of local hero General Osório (who defended the empire in the wars with Paraguay, 1864–70); the other has frozen the hapless Dom Joao VI in time. The **Chafariz do Mestre Valentim** is the city's old water source, and the area immediately around it has been excavated to reveal traces of colonial Rio's shore line.

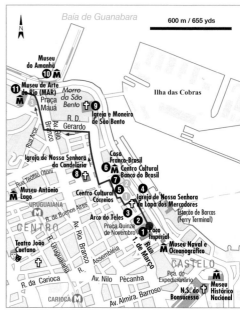

Barber shop in the Centro

A rainy day in Centro

OLD QUARTER

With your back to the bay, cross to the right of the square and enter the old world enclosed by the **Arco do Teles** ❸, an archway that goes back to 1790. Beyond it is **Travessa do Comércio**, a medieval-looking alleyway, with cobbled stones and balconies made of rickety wrought-iron work. Make a note that, in the evenings towards the end of the week, you may find informal samba gatherings here. The almost-hidden entrance to No. 17, **Casa Granado**, home of the former apothecary to the royal family, conceals still-functioning, ultramodern, open-plan offices. It's not open for visits, but around the corner, back on Rua Primeiro de Março 16, is their original store. Here you'll find a range of luxury soaps and perfumes filling a space which recreates a 19th-century pharmacy.

Rua do Ouvidor

The narrow street which crosses Travessa do Comércio is **Rua do Ouvidor**. At lunchtime and in the evenings, tables and chairs take over the entire street, with a dozen or so *botequims*, jostling side by side. Catering to young professionals from nearby offices, the place often has a lively atmosphere, particularly during weekdays.

Turning left on to Rua do Ouvidor, a few steps away is the **Igreja de Nossa Senhora da Lapa dos Mercadores** ❹ (Church of Our Lady of the Merchants; Mon–Sat 8am–2pm; free). This tiny church with ornate decoration was built by grateful merchants in 1747, and is considered a gem of Baroque architecture.

Centro Cultural Correios (CCC)

With your back to the church, head straight down the narrow street in front of you, Rua dos Mercadores. At the end, carry around a slight left turn, which becomes Rua Visconde de Itaboraí. On your right you'll pass Cais do Oriente, a good place for lunch or dinner (see page 106). Next to it on the corner is the traditional **Bar do Gengibre** ❶, a good little spot for a coffee, snack or lunch.

Across the corner on Rua Visconde de Itaboraí, 20, is a pale three-story building with a round dome, the **Centro Cultural Correios** ❺, (Post Office Cultural Center; Tue–Sun noon–7pm; free). It houses up to five temporary art exhibitions at a time, always of the highest standard, beautifully showcased by perennially creative local designers. No boring rows of badly lit oil paintings here. Hardwood floorboards are polished to a mirror-like shine, occasionally lit by shafts of sunlight from the outside world. Rare and precious glimpses of the rooftops of old Rio can be spied from the windows; and the elevator is like a giant step back in time. There's also a café, a pocket theater and an open patio where 'happenings' take place. And, of course, there's a post office.

Igreja da Nossa da Candelária

Casa França-Brasil

Leaving the Centro Cultural Correios behind you, to your right, continue on down the cobbled street until you reach the **Casa França-Brasil** ❻ (Tue–Sun noon–8pm; free), which is also on your right. It was originally designed as a trading center for local produce, but it only served this humble purpose for a mere two years and by 1821 was already being used as a meeting place for politicians, just like the Roman forum it evokes. Nowadays, it houses exhibitions of many different kinds. Inside, you will experience a surprising architectural mix of neoclassical and Renaissance styles. The ceiling is impressive, and the flagstone floor ankle-breakingly irregular, so mind your step while you are gazing upwards. Inside, there's also a reading room with an immense wooden table and **The Line Bistro** ❷.

Centro Cultural Banco do Brasil (CCBB)

Across the tiny street in front of the Casa França-Brasil, is the impressive **Centro Cultural Banco do Brasil** ❼ (Wed–Mon; 9am–9pm; free), hosting exhibits by renowned Brazilian and international artists. The former headquarters of the national bank was turned into a multi-purpose cultural center in 1989 and its success spawned several similar institutions around the city. The sheer grandiosity of the building, the wonderful natural light provided by the skylight roof, and the gracefully circular mezzanines make it a perfect backdrop for a wide variety of activities. In addition to art exhibits, these marbled halls are home to a theater, video screening rooms, a cinema, a bookshop, a concert hall and a snack bar. Treat yourself, and take the elevator – a gilded cage if ever there was one – to any of the floors.

Igreja de Nossa Senhora da Candelária

As you leave the Centro Cultural Banco do Brasil, you are faced with the awesomely wide and frantically busy **Avenida Presidente Vargas**, crossing Rua Primeiro de Março. In the center of the avenue is the imposing **Igreja de Nossa Senhora da Candelária** ❽, founded in 1609 and gradually enlarged over the centuries. The austere interior is decorated by late-19th-century walls paintings by Zeferino da Costa. On a sad note, in the 1993 Candelária Massacre, eight street children were killed by the church when the police shot at a group of about seventy. Death squads in the early nineties marked one of Rio's most violent periods, before the situation began to improve by the end of the decade.

St Benedict's Church and Monastery

Carry on down Rua Primeiro de Março, sticking to the sidewalk on the left-hand side. Cross over Rua Teófilo Otoni and Rua Visconde de Inhaúma, and you are in navy territory. Observe the number of uniform outfitters and flag makers. Shortly afterwards, Rua Primeiro de Março comes to an end. Turn left onto Rua Dom Gerardo and carry on until you reach No. 68, with a sign-

Sao Bento Monastery

Museu do Amanhã

posted road leading up the hill to the **Igreja e Mosteiro de São Bento** ❾ (St Benedict's Church and Monastery; tel: 21-2291 7122; daily 7am–6pm; free). A short walk up leads you to one of Rio's most beloved churches. As you approach the building, surrounded by trees and singing birds, the portion to the right of the magnificent church gates is the secluded workplace of the Benedictine monks who still live in cloisters here. Obviously, it is off limits for visitors.

The church is renowned for its sung masses, in the rich Gregorian tradition, and you may like to time your visit so that you can hear one, or come back another time. Early morning masses are particularly uplifting. Regular masses are held Mon–Fri 7.30am (sung) and Sunday 10am (sung) and 6.10pm, along with a range of services at other times.

The deceptively simple facade leads into an ornate and grandiose interior. One is immediately struck by the intricacy of the woodcarving and the amount of gold leaf that has been applied to the interior of the church. Each side chapel seems to outdo its neighbor in embellishment. Proceeding down the right-hand side of the church, you come across the chapel devoted to the luckless St Lawrence, roasted over glowing coals in AD 248, carrying the grille upon which he met his fiery end. The high altar is dedicated to Our Lady of Monserrat. To her right she is guarded by St Benedict and to her left, by the saint's beloved sister, St Scholastica.

It seems fitting that these holy siblings should stand forever in each other's company; while they lived, they were allowed to meet only once a year.

THE PRAÇA MAUA WATERFRONT

Leave the church and veer off to the right, through a sort of tunnel between buildings. Carry on down the hill, around 100 meters/yds, and before you is the Bay of Guanabara. Down below, jutting into the sea, is a striking glass and metal structure, the **Museu do Amanhã** ❿, (Museum of Tomorrow; Praça Mauá, 1; www.museudoamanha.org.br). This captivating museum uses interactive exhibits to show what the world might be like in the next 50 years. The ship-like building, designed by the Spanish architect Santiago Calatrava, is surrounded by a shallow pool of water. To get there, carry on down the hill to your left, and soon you'll be back at sea level. Then, head to the right and walk 200 meters/yds to Praça Mauá, the large open space by the water's edge.

This area (renamed *Porto Maravilha*, or Marvellous Port) with its waterfront, new tram system and pedestrianized streets, was completely transformed between 2014 and 2016. Starting off with the demolition of an ugly concrete flyover, the derelict (and dangerous) old port district has been turned into a very pleasant waterfront and cultural nexus, drawing local families and tourists alike.

Wander around the square and waterfront, with the Museu do Amanhã

Downtown botequim

and the stained glass windows of the white cruise ship terminal (on the left as you look at the sea). Then head over to the two pale four-story buildings (one classic and one modern), joined together by a wavy roof, on the landward side of the square.

Food and Drink

🅐 BAR DO GENGIBRE

Rua Visconde de Itaboraí, 10; tel: 21-2263 1484; daily B, L and D. $

This cozy café and *botequim* occupies a historic building and has tables on the quiet cobbled street outside. Apart from coffees and lunches, try a *batida* (sweet *cachaça* cocktail).

🅑 THE LINE BISTRO

Rua Visconde de Itaboraí, 21; tel: 21-2233 3571; www.theline.com.br; daily L. $$

Partly within the Casa França-Brasil and partly taking up and outdoors terrace, this contemporary café and bistro serves snacks and lunches, plus early evening drinks (closes at 8pm).

🅒 RESTAURANTE MAUÁ

Museu de Arte do Rio, Praça Mauá, 5; tel: 21-3031 2741; www.museudearte dorio. org.br; Tue–Thu L, Fri–Sun L and D. $$$

Brazilian dishes with a creative twist are served in a contemporary space, with huge glass windows and a panoramic view over Rio's Praça Mauá and Guanabara Bay.

The **Museu de Arte do Rio (MAR)** 🅺 (Rio Art Museum; Praça Mauá, 5; tel: 21-3031 2741; www.museudeartedorio. org.br; Tue–Sun 10am–5pm) features a range of temporary art and photographic exhibitions, with a focus on social elements of Rio through the ages. Shortly after you've paid your entrance fee, you'll see a café and gift shop (with high-quality art items) at the garden level.

From the rooftop of the modern building (the first one you enter and take the elevator up to start the tour), there are views over the port and bay. You may also be wanting something to eat or drink by this stage, in which case, try the **Restaurante Mauá** 🅒 with contemporary Brazilian cuisine and a view.

Getting back to your hotel from here is easy, with plenty of taxis passing by Praça Mauá.

RESTAURANTS

Apart from the areas and restaurants mentioned en-route, the Centro has many other options for lunch, dinner or a beer, all catering to the city's office workers. You can find all sorts of places here, including Japanese, Arab and Italian restaurants, as well as traditional *churrascarias* and hundreds of *botequims*, snack bars (*lanchonetes*) and lunchtime buffet (*comida a quilo*) options. The area around Rua do Rosário, Rua da Quitanda and Rua do Ouvidor is a particularly good bet for restaurants (see page 106).

View of Downtown

CINELÂNDIA AND LAPA

Stroll through the historic districts of Cinelândia and Lapa, with monumental architecture spanning four centuries. Visit Brazil's national library and fine arts museum, then historic churches and a modern cathedral. See samba bars and an elegant former aqueduct, ending up at 215 steps covered in colorful ceramic tiles.

DISTANCE: 3.2km (2 miles) walking
TIME: A half day
START: Theatro Municipal do Rio de Janeiro, Cinelândia
END: Cinema Odeon, Cinelândia
POINTS TO NOTE: Tue–Fri (10am–5pm) are the best days for this walking tour. Many places close on Sunday and Monday and some close on Saturday. There are plenty of refreshment stops along the way. Be aware of pickpockets, particularly in Lapa, the last half of the walk.

Occupying a space settled by the Portuguese in the 17th century, the adjoining districts of Cinelândia and Lapa are located between the skyscrapers of the Centro (Rio's Downtown), the waters of Guanabara Bay and the hills of Santa Teresa. Buildings from the early colonial period can still be seen, like the Santo Antônio Monastery, founded in 1608. It's also home to early 20th-century architecture of national importance, including a Beaux Arts-style theater, a national library and a fine arts museum, all around Cinelândia's European-looking main square. Other distinct landmarks include the pyramid-shaped municipal cathedral, built out of concrete, with 64-meter-high stained glass windows.

Just around the corner is Lapa, with its samba bars and vibrant nightlife, along with the majestic white Lapa Arches and the tile-covered Selarón Steps, created by a Chilean artist over 23 years. This walking tour is a must for those interested in architecture, culture and art.

CINELÂNDIA

Your starting point is **Cinelândia ❶**, on the edge of Rio's Downtown, which has its own metro stop and is also easily reached by taxi. Translated as 'Cinema Land' this square concentrated a large number of movie houses in the early 20th century. Officially, it's called Praça Floriano, in honor of Brazil's second president, Floriano Peixoto (ruling from 1891–4), but few *cariocas* will know that Cinelândia has another name.

Museu Nacional de Belas Artes

Surrounded by monumental buildings, and with a wide road to one side, the Avenida Rio Branco, the square looks and feels very European. This is probably what was intended when it was redeveloped in 1904, replacing an older, more colonial type of layout.

If you stand in the center of the square, the first building you'll probably notice is the opulent **Theatro Municipal do Rio de Janeiro** ❷ (tel: 21-2332 9191/2332 9220; guided tours Tue–Fri 11.30am–4pm, Sat 11am–1pm). Built in 1909, Rio's Municipal Theater has a Beaux-Arts design which closely resembles the Palais Garnier Opera House in Paris. Most striking are the copper domes and the huge golden eagle.

Inside, it is just as beautiful, with sculptured features and dazzling chandeliers. Apart from the daytime guided tours, in the evenings it hosts ballet, opera and classical music performances.

As you look at the Theatro Municipal, to the left is the **Câmara Municipal do Rio de Janeiro** ❸ in the pale neo-classical Pedro Ernesto Palace, built in 1923. This is home to the Legislature of the city of Rio, where its 51 *vereadores* (town councillors) meet to vote on laws and budgets for public services.

On the other side of the square is the **Biblioteca Nacional** ❹ (The National Library; Avenida Rio Branco 219; tel: 21-2220 9484; www.bn.br; Mon–Fri 9am–7pm; free guided or self-guided

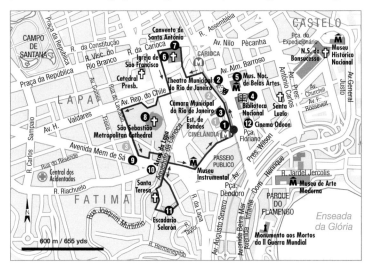

Guignard painting, MNBA

Sculptures gallery, MNBA

tours). Touted as Latin America's largest library, the Biblioteca Nacional is home to a vast collection, totaling an estimated 9 million items, including numerous rare and historic books, maps and photographs. Collections brought over from Portugal's Royal Library in 1810, plus a vast range of items chronicling 19th-century Brazil, are housed in a classic setting.

Next door is the **Museu Nacional de Belas Artes ❺** (National Fine Arts Museum; Avenida Rio Branco, 199; tel: 21-2219 8474; www.mnba.gov.br; Tue–Fri 10am–6pm, Sat–Sun noon–5pm). Home to 70,000 items, from paintings to books, this museum has the country's largest collection of Brazilian 19th-century art. Included in the collection are works by the French artist-explorers Debret and Taunay, who traveled through Brazil in the early 1800s, chronicling colonial life, people and landscapes.

Exiting the museum, by now you may be wanting a coffee or lunch. There are plenty of choices in, around and behind Cinelândia. For something to eat, options include the Brazilian bar and restaurant **Amarelinho ❶** on the square itself and the Arab **Al Kuwait ❷**, just off the square on Avenida 13 de Maio.

SÃO FRANCISCO CHURCH

From the museums of Cinelândia, head one block up Avenida 13 de Maio, with the Theatro Municipal on your right, then turn left on the busy Avenida República do Chile. As you walk, you'll see the **Igreja de São Francisco ❻** (St Francis Church; Mon–Fri 9am–noon, 1–4pm) up on a hill on your right. Head across the small park and then either go up the steps or take the elevator at the base of the hill. Its long-winded official name is the *Igreja Venerável Ordem Terceira São Francisco Penitência* and it was built between 1657 and 1733. Its facade is simple, so once you're inside, you're bound to be struck by the highly-decorated gilded carvings, covering every available space in shiny gold.

Next door is the **Convento de Santo Antônio ❼** (Monastery of Saint Anthony; Mon–Fri 8am–6pm, Sat–Sun 8am–11am). Inaugurated in 1608, this was the original building on the hill (called the Morro de Santo Antônio). This piece of higher land was granted to Franciscan monks as a better option compared to the low-lying seafront, where they had been since arriving in the early 1500s, with the first Portuguese navigators. Given the historical importance of this place of worship, you'll be surprised to see a very simple, almost run-down, interior: a contrast to its ornate neighbor, the Igreja de São Francisco. Scheduled visits which only take place only on Thursdays from 11am–12.20pm (tel: 21-2262 1029) take you into areas usually not seen, like the imperial mausoleum and the friar's dining room.

Back on Avenida República do Chile, cross over and keep following the road in the same direction, up a slight rise.

Catedral Metropolitana

On your left, you'll pass the rubik's cube-like **Petrobras building**, belonging to the national state-run oil company, which fell into disrepute in 2015 as a result of a massive corruption scandal involving its directors, politicians and large firms in the construction and oil sector. Not only did it damage its own reputation, but also that of Brazil, helping to jump-start a recession in Latin America's largest economy.

Keep going until you see a huge concrete pyramid on your left. This is the **São Sebastião Metropolitan Cathedral** ❽ (Avenida República do Chile, 245; tel: 21-2240 2669; www.catedral.com.br; daily 7am–5pm). Inaugurated in 1979, it has a huge circular interior, is 75 meters/yds tall and has a capacity of 5,000 people seated or 20,000 standing. Four massive stained glass windows span 64 meters (210ft), from the floor to the ceiling. Although not to everyone's taste, and quite different to any other cathedral, its sheer size and audacity impresses.

LAPA

Once back outside, keep heading down Avenida República do Chile and then turn left up Rua do Lavradio (if you turn right, you'll reach a series of bars hosting live samba in the evenings, including **Rio Scenarium** at Rua do Lavradio, 20; Tue–Sat 7.30pm–3am). As you walk along Rua do Lavradio, notice all the small shops selling rustic wooden furniture and antiques.

After two blocks, you'll hit **Avenida Mem de Sá** ❾, the heart of Lapa, Rio's liveliest bar district and the place to come in the evenings for live samba bands. If you come during the day, most places will be closed. All down the street, double-story houses from the early 20th century have been transformed into *botecos*: Rio's answer to English and Irish pubs, with *chope* draft lagers and hearty Brazilian pub grub. When it comes to searching for samba bands, there's plenty of choice, with some places offering free entry, others a cover charge. One place which is open during the day is the traditional restaurant **Bar Brasil** ❸.

Turn left on Avenida Mem de Sá and then after 100 meters/yds you'll reach the Carioca Aqueduct, commonly known as the **Arcos da Lapa** ❿. Spanning 270 meters (886ft) across a large open space, this structure, with 42 double arches painted white, was inaugurated in 1750. Up until the end of the 1800s, it brought fresh water to Rio's built-up area, including Largo da Carioca below the Convento de Santo Antônio. The water came from the source of the Carioca River up in the Santa Teresa hills. As the city grew and the Carioca River became less dependable, the aqueduct was transformed (in 1896) into a bridge for a new *bondinho* tram, linking the Centro with manor houses in Santa Teresa.

Pass under the Arcos da Lapa and then follow it (with the arches to your

Live samba at Rio Scenarium

right and the open square behind you). Head towards a narrow road, the Rua Joaquim Silva, hemmed in by old, run-down houses. Follow the road around a bend to the left and pass a series of local bars. Another 100 meters/yds further on, to your right is the **Escadaria Selarón ⓫**. Known in English as the 'Selarón Steps' they're named after the Chilean artist Jorge Selarón. Around 1990 he began renovating a few dilapidated steps in front of his house. It soon became an obsession and gradually (23 years later) all 215 steps on this hillside were covered in ceramic tiles, with all sorts of vibrant colors and patterns.

In total, Selarón used over 2,000 tiles from 60 countries, including ones sourced from construction sites, donated by visitors and painted by him. It was completely self-funded and he was constantly running out of money, so he had to keep selling more of his paintings to keep going. In 2013, he was found dead in mysterious circumstances on his steps, his life's passion.

Head to the top of the steps, a photographer's delight, and then turn right to come back down via the Ladeira de Santa Teresa, which rejoins the Arcos da Lapa. If you want to head back to the bars of Lapa, turn left back down Avenida Mem de Sá. Otherwise, catch a taxi to head home, or to get back to the Cinelândia metro, follow Avenida Mem de Sá to the right, away from the arches, and turn left at Rua do Passeio, keeping the green open space, Praça Passeio Público, on your right. Reach the 1926 **Cinema Odeon ⓬**, on the corner of Cinelândia.

Food and Drink

❶ AMARELINHO
Praça Floriano, 55; tel: 21-2240 8434; www.amarelinhocinelandia.com.br; daily L and D. $
Founded in 1921, this is a traditional and simply-decorated spot, with tables on the square, serving *chopes* (draft beers), appetizers, steaks and hearty *feijoada*.

❷ AL KUWAIT
Avenida 13 de Maio, 23; tel: 21-2240 1114; www.alkuwait.com.br; Mon–Fri B, L and D. $$
Around since the 1950s, this simply-decorated Arab restaurant serves *kibes*, *kaftas*, stuffed vine leaves and lamb, as well as Brazilian-style grilled meats and seafood.

❸ BAR BRASIL
Avenida Mem de Sá, 90, Lapa; tel: 21-2509 5943; www.barbrasil.com.br; Mon–Sat L and D. $$
Founded in 1907 by Austrians, this traditional neighborhood bar and restaurant serves Germanic dishes, like pork cutlets, sausages and sauerkraut, along with cold beers, in unfussy surrounds.

COPACABANA

Stroll along one of the world's most famous beaches, starting off at a little-visited hilltop fort surrounded by tropical forest. Stop for drink at the iconic Copacabana Palace Hotel, then continue to the end of the beach, where there are colorful fishing boats and a second fort, with cafés on the seawall and a panoramic view.

DISTANCE: 6km (3.5 miles)
TIME: 4 hours
START: Forte do Leme
END: Forte de Copacabana
POINTS TO NOTE: Do not undertake this route on Mondays, as the forts will be closed. The 4km (2.5-mile) stretch along Copacabana offers no shade, so the walk is best done with a hat and suntan lotion, and at the start of the day (the forts open at 9.30am, but close at 4.30pm). An alternative to walking the entire length of the beach is to catch a taxi in the parts suggested.

Copacabana is perhaps one of the world's most famous beaches. Without doubt, it's one of Rio's better known landmarks, along with Ipanema, the Sugarloaf and Corcovado. For most of Rio's history it was an undeveloped 4km (2.5-mile) stretch of sand, backed by dunes and vegetation. Then the 20th century came and Copacabana's iconic hotel,

the Copacabana Palace Hotel, was built. Soon after, the entire stretch was densely-packed apartment blocks. When most *cariocas* and tourists come here, they head straight for the sand, the waves and the kiosks. Less visited are the two forts at either end of the beach: one up on a hill and surrounded by forest, the other at the water's edge with cafés along a seawall. You'll see all sorts of sports being played on the beach and all sorts of beachwear. It's certainly a good place to people watch. On the western side, you'll even find a small section with colorful fishing boats and fresh fish for sale. For a first-time visit to Rio, Copacabana is a must, and it's the sort of place which keeps drawing people back.

FORTE DO LEME

The walk starts off at the far left side of Copacabana Beach as you look at the sea. To be precise, this part of the beach is known as Leme. Although it's all the same 4km (2.5-mile) stretch of sand,

Copacabana by night

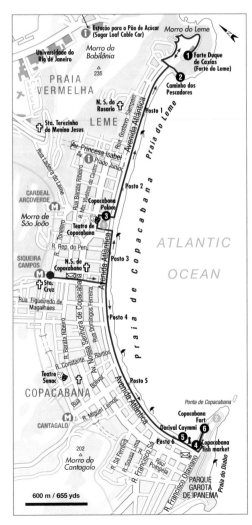

the road which divides Copacabana from Leme is Avenida Princesa Isabel: the main thoroughfare which goes through a tunnel to Botafogo.

You'll notice a tall rounded granite hill at this end of the beach, with a fort on top. This is your starting point, so head along the promenade of the beach until you get to the end. Behind the beach is the Almirante Duque de Noronha Square, with benches and exercise machines. Just behind this is a ticket booth and the entrance to the **Forte do Leme ❶** (Leme Fort; tel: 21-3223 5076; Tue–Sun 9.30am–4.30pm; self-guided visits; free for over-60s and under-10s). Everyone knows it as Forte do Leme, but officially, it's called **Forte Duque de Caxias**, a name which it received in 1934, in honor of an eminent 19th-century politician and army officer. The 'Iron Duke' fought many battles, including the 1823 Brazilian War of Independence and the

Copacabana's famous promenade

1835–45 Ragamuffin War (*Revolução Farroupilha*), a secessionist movement in the southern state of Rio Grande do Sul.

The original defence system built in 1776, when there were rumors of an imminent Spanish invasion, was baptized Forte do Vigia (Lookout Fort). The invasion which did indeed happen in 1777, took place not in Rio, but in the south of the Portuguese colony of Brazil. The Spaniards invaded Ilha de Santa Catarina (home of present-day Florianópolis) and recaptured Colónia do Sacramento, a Portuguese-held outpost on the River Plate, which would later become part of Uruguay.

The Forest of Forte do Leme

Just past the ticket booth, pass the barracks and buildings of the **Centro de Estudos de Pessoal**, a military training centre for 18-year-old conscripts. Just behind this, the path enters the forest and the temperature immediately drops.

The cobbled path gently climbs into the **Mata Atlântica** forest. There are plaques along the way describing this ecosystem and its native wildlife. In this forest, 89 of Rio's 481 bird species have been recorded. Examples include the *Sangue de Boi* (a deep-red Brazilian tanager) and *Saracura-do-Mato* (the ground-dwelling Slaty-breasted wood rail). To increase your chances of seeing birdlife, go slowly and quietly. What you will definitely see are *saguis* (also called *micos*, or marmosets), which are not at all shy. As the path climbs there are occasional glimpses of Copacabana Beach down below. Further on, you will see the mouth of Guanabara Bay and the Sugarloaf looming above it.

In 1987, a reforestation project was initiated, which led to the planting of 11,000 native tree seedlings. In 1990, the **Área de Proteção Ambiental (APA) do Morro de Leme**, was founded. This conservation area also included Cotunduba Island, near the mouth of the Bay, and Morro do Urubu, a hillside beside the *Morro da Babilônia* favela. Photos taken at three-year intervals show light green grassy slopes quickly turning into deep green ones. The same process was undertaken in a separate project for *Morro da Babilônia* itself bringing the total reforested area to 124 acres (50 hectares).

Forte do Leme

After 20 minutes, you'll reach the top of the hill and the Fort, with panoramic views of Copacabana Beach. Through a colorful gateway marking the entrance to Duque de Caxias Fort proper, you'll enter a defensive system with solid ramparts and massive howitzers. Walking around the walls, views of the Sugarloaf and Atlantic Ocean are impressive. A small museum by the entrance describes the Fort's history and its role in countless military episodes during this

Strolling along the beach

young country's existence. Take time to take in the views and the silence before you head back down.

LEME BEACH

When you reach the entrance of the fort, back down at beach level, you'll see kiosks along the base of the rock face. Beyond this is a narrow pathway cut into the rock, above the sea. This is the **Caminho dos Pescadores** ❷ (Fishermen's Trail), where local anglers congregate to cast their lines into the rough sea below. From the trail there is a panoramic view of Copacabana Beach and you may also see surfers catching waves just below you. Looking towards land, note the *Morro da Babilônia* favela rising steeply behind apartment blocks. If you're interested in seeing a favela (see page 52), this is one of the safest and access to it is up the *Ladeira Ary Barroso* road, which starts a couple of blocks back from the beach. If you have time, head up there now, or come back for another visit.

COPACABANA BEACH

Walking along the promenade, past beachside kiosks selling coconut water and fast food, note the iconic wavy pattern at your feet. Created in contrasting black and white, out of small pieces of marble imported from Portugal, and then hammered one by one into place, the idea was very Portuguese. Go to Lisbon and you'll see the same sort of paving and you won't be surprised to hear that this sort of paving is called *calçada portuguesa*. The wavy pattern itself developed over time, from when it first appeared

A Day at the Beach

Rio's beaches are a major draw for tourists and a year-round playground for the city's residents. They're at their liveliest in the summer holidays (Dec–Feb), when almost every square inch of sand is occupied. Along the promenade kiosks sell *água de coco* (coconut water), beers and snacks, while on the beach *barracas* (tents) rent out parasols and deck chairs. Hawkers sell *mate* (iced tea), *Biscoitos Globo* (fluffy manioc flour snacks) and *esfihas* (Arab pastries), along with sarongs and straw hats.

At the back of the beach, games of volleyball take place, while at the water's edge, *altinho* is a skillful game where small groups keep a compact ball up in the air, just using their feet, thighs and heads. By Copacabana Fort, stand-up paddleboards (SUPs) are rented by the hour. At the end of the day, everyone claps the setting sun, the beach empties and Copacabana's juice bars and *botecos* (carioca-style pubs) start to fill.

Copacabana beach

in 1906 to the final 1970 design by Burle Marx, a renowned artist and landscape gardener. The entire length of the beach is 4km (2.5 miles), so you have plenty of time to photograph Brazil's most famous walkway.

Copacabana Palace Hotel

After approximately 1km (0.6 miles), you'll see the eight-story **Copacabana Palace Hotel** ❸ on your right. Built in 1923 in an elegant Art Deco style, painted white and taking up almost an entire block, Rio's most famous hotel regally looks out to sea. Apart from luxury suites, the hotel has four bars and restaurants open to the public, including Cipriani, for Italian cuisine (see page 108), the Mee (serving contemporary Asian dishes), a piano bar and the poolside **Pérgula Restaurant** ❶, a casual, but sophisticated, spot for a drink or light meal. Within the hotel, and adjoining it along the street, there are high-end souvenir and jewelry shops. Worth a visit is Amsterdam Sauer, to the right as you head out of the hotel. Upstairs is an impressive collection of stone-cut parrots perched atop huge shiny semi-precious stones and crystals. Shop attendants are friendly without being pushy. Sculptures cost upwards of US$500.

Western End of Copacabana Beach

The next stop is 3km (2 miles) further along the beach, at the western end, so this might be a good chance to catch a taxi from the Copacabana Palace Hotel or nearby. As you head along the beach, notice all the sporting action – joggers, people on their bikes, surfers, volleyball and soccer players. Perhaps most impressive of all is *futevôlei* (footvolley), a version of volleyball where hands cannot be used. Instead it's all feet, head and shoulders, requiring ultra-fit players who usually play in pairs. Like many sports, footvolley developed over time but Octavio Moraes (1923–2009), who played for Botafogo, one of Rio's soccer teams, is generally regarded as the person who invented it. That was back in the 1960s and the place in which it was invented was Copacabana Beach itself.

Continue until you reach the end of Copacabana Beach, where you'll see colorful fishing boats and the small **Copacabana fish market** ❹. The best time to find fresh fish is in the mornings. On calm days, the sea in this part of Copacabana is like a lagoon and it's a popular spot for stand-up paddle boarding, with a series of places on the sand to rent the boards.

On the walkway, notice the **statue of Dorival Caymmi** ❺ (1914–2008) standing with a guitar in hand. He was a renowned Brazilian musician and one of the early contributors to the bossa nova movement, which took place in the 1950s in Rio.

Copacabana Fort   *Café 18 do Forte*

Copacabana Fort

To reach the entrance to **Copacabana Fort ❻** (Praça Coronel Eugênio Franco, 1; tel: 21-2287 3781; www. fortedecopacabana.com; Tue–Sun 10am–6pm, cafés inside are open until 8pm) continue walking just past the fishing boats and as the main road curves to the right, turn left through the gates with military personnel into the fort. The low rocky headland, site of the present-day fort, was originally home to a church, built by a Bolivian trader who survived a shipwreck in these treacherous waters. Inside the church was placed a replica of *Our Lady of Copacabana*, the patron saint of Bolivia. Eventually, Copacabana lent its name to this part of Rio (which back then was undeveloped). The fort itself was only started in 1908, taking six years to complete.

The pathway heads along the waterfront, past cannons, with a view of Copacabana Beach and Sugarloaf Mountain behind Forte do Leme. Along the entire beachfront there are tall apartment blocks and in one section these are backed by the *Morro do Cantagalo* favela on the steep hillside. As you continue, you'll pass a couple of cafés with outdoor tables overlooking this panorama. Confeitaria Colombo is a branch of the iconic establishment in Rio's Centro (see page 107), and just beyond it is **Café 18 do Forte ❷**. There's also a museum recounting Brazil's history from a military perspective and recreating scenes from specific battles and wars. At the end of the walkway, you reach the massive dome-shaped fort. Visitors can walk onto the rooftop and through tunnels where you'll see cannons and prison-like rooms. The fort was used through the years, spanning both world wars and the post-War World II military dictatorship, which came to an end in 1985.

Food and Drink

❶ PÉRGULA RESTAURANT

Copacabana Palace Hotel, Avenida Atlântica 1702; tel: 21-2508 7070; daily B, L and D. $$
Apart from coffees, beers and cocktails, this spot offers brunch on Sundays and daily buffet lunches, as well as light meals. Most people come here for the setting, with outdoor tables by the hotel's elegant pool.

❷ CAFÉ 18 DO FORTE

Forte de Copacabana; tel: 21-2523 0171; www.cafe18doforte.com; Tue–Sun B, L and D. $$
Set within the grounds of Copacabana Fort and with outdoor tables on the seafront, this is a tranquil spot to enjoy coffee and sandwiches, plus typical Brazilian appetizers and dishes. The view takes in Copacabana Beach, Sugarloaf Mountain and the coastline beyond Rio.

Volleyball match

IPANEMA AND LAGOA

This walk introduces you to some of the highlights of Ipanema, including its squares, Sunday markets and, of course, the beach. You'll have a chance to see a gemstone museum and eat in a local boteco, before you reach a lakeside walking trail. Pop into Flamengo, a famous soccer club, then end the tour in a café amidst tropical gardens.

DISTANCE: 4km (2.5 miles) walking, plus a 3.2km (2-mile) taxi ride
TIME: 4 hours
START: Praça General Osório, Ipanema
END: Parque Lage, Jardim Botânico
POINTS TO NOTE: The entire route can be walked, but we recommend a taxi for the last section. It is best done in the morning, when it is cooler and the sun less strong. There are plenty of refreshment stops along the way. If undertaken on a Sunday, you'll see the Hippie Fair at the start of the walk, but miss out on the Amsterdam Sauer Museum (Mon–Fri 9am–7pm, Sat until 2pm).

Ipanema, a virgin beach and neighborhood in the 19th century, developed in the 1960s into what you see today: tall residential blocks, shops and cafés behind a sandy playground dotted with tanned bodies and kiosks selling coconut water. As tourism increased and the 1964 hit 'The Girl from Ipanema' was released, Ipanema suddenly became one of the world's most famous beaches, synonymous with the *cidade maravilhosa*, the marvellous city of Rio. For apartment-dwelling *cariocas*, the beaches are a place to enjoy the sunshine, practice sports, meet friends. The saying goes that these sandy stretches are the most democratic places in Brazil: where people of all backgrounds mix, in a very relaxed, down-to-the-swimwear, sort of way.

A few blocks inland from the beach, Ipanema is bordered by another body of water: the calm Lagoa Rodrigo de Freitas lagoon. There's a 7.5km (5-mile) cycle path and walking trail all the way around it, with views up steep forested slopes, including Corcovado, the 710-meter (2,329ft) -high mountain, topped by the Christ the Redeemer statue. Around the lake are rowing clubs, including Flamengo, which is now much more famous for its soccer team. At the back of the Lagoa are the traditional Gávea and Jardim Botânico neighborhoods, with Rio's Jockey Club, the Botanic Gardens and the last stop in this tour: Parque Lage, with rambling tropical gardens and a palatial 1920s Italian-style manor house.

Twilight on Ipanema Beach

IPANEMA

Start off at **Praça General Osório** ❶, a leafy square with its own metro stop (General Osório), named after an eminent 19th-century military commander who led Brazilian troops in various regional wars involving Brazil's southern neighbors. Every Sunday since 1968, the square has hosted the **Feira Hippie**, a lively arts and crafts market where you can find leatherwork, baskets, brightly-colored paintings and much more. The 'Hippie Fair' runs from 7am to 7pm and is a good place to stock up on authentic handmade souvenirs. In the southwest corner of the square look out for a food stall selling *acarajé*, a typical snack from the state of Bahia, consisting of a black-eyed pea fritter with a spicy filling, topped by dried shrimp.

Head down Rua Teixeira de Melo to **Ipanema Beach** ❷, which is only one block away. When you arrive at the promenade overlooking the sand, note the black-and-white marble paving, whose geometric rounded squares are a contrast to Copacabana's wavy design. Straight ahead of you is one of the world's most famous beaches, usually crowded with beachgoers. Out to sea, the rounded granite islands are the Cagarras, a nature reserve home to a wide range of seabirds, whose excretions over millennia have streaked the rocks white.

Ipanema is an indigenous word meaning 'stinky lake', but this wasn't the original name for this neighborhood and beach. Instead, the name derives from the wealthy Baron of Ipanema (who hailed from the interior of São Paulo state). When he bought the land back in the 19th century it was completely undeveloped: just a few farmhouses. Eventually he split it up, selling it off in blocks for the construction of houses. For the first half of the 20th century it remained a quiet residential area, but then came the construction boom of the 1950s and '60s. Tall apartment blocks sprung up, creating the Ipanema we know today.

Standing on the beachfront promenade, look left and approximately 500 meters/yds away, the rocky headland is called **Arpoador**. Its name in English means 'Harpooner', in reference to former whaling days. Nowadays, it's a favorite spot for fishing and watching the sun set.

Look in the other direction, to the right, and at the far end of the beach, approximately 2km (1.2 miles) away, are the steep twin peaks of **Dois Irmãos**, whose highest point is 533 meters (1,749ft) above sea level. A popular (and not too difficult) 1–2 hour hiking route around the back of the mountain reaches the summit. The starting point of the walk (which is best accompanied by a guide) is the top of **Vidigal**, the favela which takes up the lower seaward flanks of Dois Irmãos. Vidigal itself is an example of a pacified shanty town, where heavy police presence has largely removed the control once held by drug lords. This, added to its enviable location and panoramic views of Rio's iconic coastline, has made it a trendy up-and-coming spot, with hilltop

Garota de Ipanema

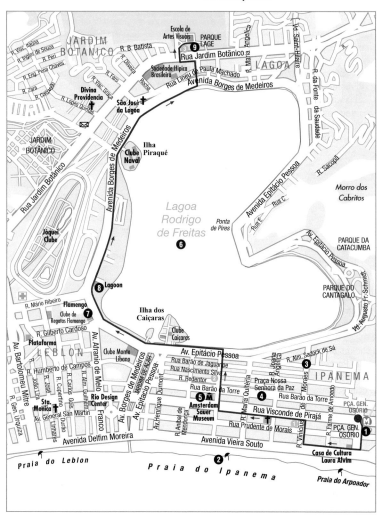

Surfers on Ipanema beach

Bag shopping on Visconde de Pirajá

bars and backpacker hostels. Unfortunately, the resulting steep rise in property prices has a negative flipside. Poorer families can now longer afford the higher rents asked by their landlords, and are thus forced to move out to more distant favelas with lower rents.

Ipanema Beach, which becomes **Leblon Beach** the other side of the Jardim do Allah canal, is one continuous 2.5km (1.5-mile) stretch. However, it's divided into imaginary sections, according to the *Postos* (lifeguard posts) along the way. Each Posto has its own culture, so in Rio when you say you're going to the beach, you generally say which specific Posto you're going to. Starting at the eastern end, Posto 7 at Arpoador is for surfers and teenagers from the nearby Cantagalo favela. Posto 8 is gay-friendly, with rainbow flags and a party vibe. Posto 9 is an alternative, left-wing and intellectual sort of place. Posto 10 attracts beach sports enthusiasts: volleyball players galore. Posto 11, on the Leblon side, is for millionaires and billionaires. By the time you get to Posto 12 at the western end, you'll see mothers, toddlers and baby-changing facilities. There's a spot for everyone.

Vinícius de Moraes

Walk along the beachfront for two blocks, careful to avoid speedy bikers on the cycle path, then turn up **Rua Vinícius de Moraes** ❸, which is named after the renowned *carioca* poet, playwright and music writer. Vinícius de Moraes, who lived in Ipanema, is most famous for writing the lyrics to the 1964 bossa nova hit 'Garota de Ipanema' (The Girl from Ipanema), in collaboration with other now-famous musicians: Tom Jobim, Stan Getz, João Gilberto and Astrud Gilberto. After one block on your left, notice the *boteco* **Garota de Ipanema** ❶, named after the song and an old drinking spot of Moraes and Tom Jobim. Continue for another block and then turn left on Rua Visconde de Pirajá, Ipanema's busy shop-lined street.

Visconde de Pirajá and Garcia d'Avila

Walk along Rua Visconde de Pirajá for a block until you reach **Praça Nossa Senhora da Paz** ❹, one of Ipanema's original squares, now with a metro stop. Along the main road you'll see flower stalls and the white twin-towered **Nossa Senhora da Paz church**, built in 1918 and housing the same-named statuette, originally brought over from France and paraded down the street from Copacabana until she reached her final destination.

Walk two more blocks until you reach Rua Garcia d'Avila and take a right. After 50 meters/yds you'll reach the **Amsterdam Sauer Museum** ❺ (Rua Garcia d'Avila, 105; tel: 21-2512 1132; www.amsterdamsauer.com.br; Mon–Fri 10am–7pm, Sat until 2pm). Inside, you'll find a private collection of 3,000 gemstones, mostly from Brazil, and be able to watch craftsmen create pieces of jewelry behind glass windows. At the end of the visit, you'll enter the store of Amsterdam Sauer, a company founded

Lagoa Rodrigo de Freitas

in 1941 by Jules Sauer. An 18-year-old immigrant who left France penniless, he made his fortune by finding and exploiting new sources of gemstones in the inland state of Minas Gerais.

Turning left out of the shop, continue up prosperous Rua Garcia d'Avila, where you'll pass boutique shops and bistros. For something more typically *carioca*, try **Restaurante Paz e Amor ②**.

LAGOA

It's another two blocks up Rua Garcia d'Avila to **Lagoa Rodrigo de Freitas ❻**. Usually shortened to Lagoa (which is also the name of the neighborhood on the eastern shore), this is the large lagoon at the heart of Rio's wealthy Zona Sul (Southern Zone): the place where Ipanema, Leblon, Gávea, Lagoa and Jardim Botânico converge. Cross over the tree-lined avenue, Avenida Epitácio Pessoa, to the lakeside, where a walking trail and cycle path follow the 7.5km (5-mile) -long shore all the way around the Lagoa. Joggers, cyclists and dog-walkers are usually out in full force. At weekends, rowers and sailors take to the lagoon. These waters were also chosen as the venue for the rowing and sprint canoeing races in the **Rio 2016 Olympics**. There are some lakeside cafés along the way and magnificent vistas all around. From this very spot, you'll see forest-covered Corcovado Mountain rising up 710 meters (2,329ft), topped by the Christ the Redeemer statue.

Flamengo Sports Club

As you look at the lake, turn left (west), following the trail in a clockwise direction for 600 meters/yds. On the way, you'll pass an island across a narrow channel on your right. This is **Ilha dos Caiçaras**, a country club for Rio's elite. Shortly after, you'll pass some public tennis courts by the trail and then reach a couple of rowing clubs by the water's edge down below (this is the finishing line for the Olympic races). To your left, across the road, is **Flamengo ❼**, the sports club officially called *Clube de Regatas do Flamengo*. Home to what is probably Brazil's most famous and successful soccer team, Flamengo was founded in 1895 as a rowing club. Nowadays, the club also has swimming, basketball and volleyball teams, but soccer is by far the most popular sport, attracting the bulk of Flamengo's 40 million official supporters. The original stadium is here, but is no longer used for matches, as it's far too small. As a visitor, you're allowed in to the shop, which is full of striped red and black sports gear. Through the back, you can take a peek at the sports facilities. As an aside, Rio's other soccer teams are Fluminense, Vasco and Botafogo: the rivalry is intense and the passions are high.

Continuing another 100 meters/yds along the lakeshore, you'll reach **Lagoon ❽**, a modern restaurant complex featuring a range of contemporary dining options with panoramic views of the Lagoa.

Café du Lage

PARQUE LAGE

At this point, if you're not wanting to walk 3.5km (2.2 miles), catch a taxi (from the lakeshore side) and ask for Parque Lage. The most common route for the taxi driver to take is along the lakeshore, continuing in the same clockwise direction you've been walking. After 3km (2 miles), he or she will turn inland to reach **Parque Lage ❾** (Rua Jardim Botânico, 414; daily 8am–5pm). In some ways, this is a small version of the Botanic Gardens, which are approximately 1km (0.6 miles) away. Once the residence of late 19th-century industrialist Enrique Lage, the Parque Lage comprises 129 acres (52 hectares), most of it steep forested slopes. Nearer road level are pathways, ponds and stone-built gazebos in elegant tropical gardens, originally designed in 1840 by the British landscape designer John Tyndale. If you look up, there is a dramatic view to Christ the Redeemer, atop Corcovado Mountain, way above you. Coincidentally, a steep 3-hour walking trail up Corcovado starts here. In the grounds, the elegant manor house, which takes center stage, was remodeled by the Italian architect, Mario Vodret, in the 1920s. Inside, there is a small visual arts center and the **Café du Lage ❸** around a relaxing courtyard pool.

Food and Drink

❶ GAROTA DE IPANEMA

Rua Vinícius de Moraes, 49, Ipanema; tel: 21-2523 3787; daily L and D. $$

Although at the time it was called Bar Veloso, this drinking spot is where the famous musicians and writers, Tom Jobim and Vinícius de Moraes, used to hang out. It's named after their most famous song, 'Garota de Ipanema', and occasionally it hosts live bossa nova music upstairs. Otherwise, most people come to this *boteco* for *bolinhos de bacalhau* (cod fritters), *caipirinhas* and *picanha* steaks.

❷ RESTAURANTE PAZ E AMOR

Rua Garcia d'Avila, 173, Ipanema; tel: 21-2523 0496; www.restaurantepazeamor.com; daily B, L and D. $$

Aptly named the 'Love and Peace Restaurant', this is a tranquil *boteco* with a veranda overlooking a quiet tree-lined street. Traditionally-dressed waiters serve cold *chopes* (draft beers), appetizers like *pastéis* and huge portions of steak with fries, *feijoada* and Brazilian sandwiches like *baurus*.

❸ BISTRÔ PLAGE

Rua Jardim Botânico, 414; tel: 21-2226 8125; daily B, L and D. $$

This feels like a little corner of Europe, where you can enjoy a cappuccino with fresh bread and jam, while sitting around the courtyard pool of an Italian-looking manor house. At lunchtime there are sandwiches, salads and omelets. From Monday to Thursday, it's also open until 10.30pm, serving drinks and appetizers.

Favela rooftops

ZONA NORTE

Use taxis or the train to visit three distinct attractions in the Zona Norte (Rio's northern suburbs). Step into the iconic Maracanã Stadium, the country's most famous soccer venue, then take a gondola high over the Complexo do Alemão shantytown. Finish off in a lively indoor fair, celebrating the culture of Northeast Brazil.

DISTANCE: 16km (10 miles) taxi or train

TIME: A full day

START: Teleférico do Complexo do Alemão, Zona Norte

END: Feira de São Cristóvão

POINTS TO NOTE: All sights on this journey are open Tue–Sat, but the ideal day to undertake it is on a Saturday. This is when the Feira Nordestina is liveliest (especially in the evenings) and you might catch a soccer match at the Maracanã. On Sundays, the Teleférico do Complexo do Alemão is closed. On Mondays, the Feira Nordestina is closed. The entire route is done by cable car, taxi and/or train.

This route takes you into the the Zona Norte, the Northern Zone, which most tourists only see when driving between the international airport and the Zona Sul (home to Rio's beaches, iconic sights and famous neighborhoods). The northern suburbs, on flatlands away from the coast, cover a huge area, from the traditional middle-class neighborhoods of Tijuca and Maracanã to sprawling low-income communities in the Complexo do Alemão and beyond. A visit here gives an insight into the other side of Rio, which few people spend time getting to know. Specifically, in this itinerary, you'll learn about favelas, Brazilian soccer and the culture of Northeastern Brazil.

THE TELEFÉRICO

Be aware of pickpockets, especially at the train stations and at the Feira Nordestina. When it comes to places to eat, you'll find plenty of snack bars along the way, plus a huge number of Northeastern bars and restaurants in the Feira de São Cristóvão at the end of the tour (you may want to save up your hunger for this).

There are two ways to get to the gondolas of the **Teleférico do Complexo do Alemão** ❶ (Mon–Fri 6am–8pm, Sat 8am–6pm), by the **Bonsucesso train station** in the Zona Norte. The first option is by taxi, which from the Zona Sul (such as Copacabana or Ipanema), should cost no more than US$25 (4 people maximum

Cable cars over the Complexo do Alemão

per taxi). The second way to get there is from the Central metro and train station on Avenida Presidente Vargas in Rio's Downtown. If you catch a metro from Copacabana to Central and then the train to Bonsucesso, you'll pay around US$2 per person in total. Once at the Bonsucesso train station, you're at the start of the Teleférico do Complexo do Alemão gondola system.

A Gondola Over the Favelas

Inaugurated in 2011 and connecting Bonsucesso to five successive gondola stations (ending at Palmeiras), this 3.5km (2.2-mile) journey was built for residents of the sprawling hillside **Complexo do Alemão** favelas. An arduous journey to get home was suddenly made easier and cheaper for residents. Prices have been kept low: less than the cost of a local bus or metro ticket.

For the tourist, this is a way to see a favela up-close, without doing an organized favela tour. It's also safer than wandering around a favela on your own: here you're in the safety of a gondola flying over the houses. A word of caution: you should still be aware of pickpockets on the metro and at the stations; and you shouldn't wander around the favela without a guide.

The journey really does give an insight into the structure of a favela: a mosaic of buildings built mainly in bare brick, others painted in bright colors, and all interconnected by a web of narrow roads and alleyways. Down below you'll see children playing on rooftops, motorbikes whizzing through the

streets and hear funk (pronounced funky) music wafting up. On bare grassy slopes you may see grazing horses. Look around you to see Guanabara Bay and the Serra dos Orgãos Mountains behind it. On a steep granite hill, with 328 steps, catch sight of the Penha Sanctuary, built in 1728 and with pointed twin towers. In the other direction, towards the Zona Sul, is Corcovado Mountain.

There are 152 gondolas and it takes 16 minutes to get to Palmeiras station at the end. Once you get there, you'll find snack bars serving typical Northeastern food (reflecting the origin of many of Rio's favela dwellers). On the walls, see graffiti by local artists. At weekends, there's often live Brazilian music: come on a Saturday or during the summer and you'll probably hear samba.

Complexo do Alemão

The Complexo do Alemão is a group of favelas which have merged together into a huge area, home to an estimated 70,000 people. In the 1920s, the land was largely rural and owned by a Pole, Leonard Kaczmarkiewicz, who, because of his fair looks (and perhaps unpronounceable surname) was given the common nickname *Alemão* ('German'; the other nickname for fair people in Brazil is Russo, 'Russian'). As Rio grew and immigrants arrived, favelas developed, replacing once rural areas.

Officially, the favela was 'pacified' (see page 52) in 2010, when a police operation supposedly flushed out drug lords. Today, you'll see a heavy police presence

and fortified posts: the Police Pacification Units (UPPs). The reality is that it's a huge area and it's been impossible to eradicate gang-related crime. Criminals, if they didn't flee to another favela, just hid and things went underground. Drugs continue to be sold in alleyways, guns are hidden under mattresses, police are bribed to look the other way and shoot-outs are a regular occurrence. It's a precarious situation and the favelas of the Zona Norte, including the Complexo do Alemão, are notoriously violent.

The gondola system is generally a secure bubble for visitors, but remain watchful as the situation can change at any time: speak to a reliable source before undertaking the journey, or come with a guide.

MARACANÃ

To get to **Maracanã** ❷, Brazil's legendary soccer stadium, from Bonsucesso train station, either catch the 10-minute metro train (around US$1) in the direction of Central (getting off at Maracanã), or a taxi (around US$10). There are two options for visiting Maracanã, (Avenida Presidente Castelo Branco; tel: 21-3547 7944; www.maracana.com): either the daytime tour (9am–5pm) of the grounds or a match at the end of the day.

The daytime tour of the grounds involves hourly guided tours for around US$10 or self-guided for around US$5. On match days the last tour is 4 hours before kick-off. Tickets can be bought at

Maracaná soccer stadium

the entrance by the Maracanã metro or online. You'll visit the press box, locker room and walk on to the pitch. There's also a museum showcasing the history of the stadium and highlighting soccer legends, like Pelé and Mané Garrincha. For children, there's a child-friendly tour called the Maraca Jr.

A second option is to come to Maracanã to watch a soccer match. Games are played year-round and most take place on Saturdays and Sundays, with others on Wednesdays and Thursdays; and they're mainly in the afternoons and evenings. Admission prices for matches are around US$10–20. Check the website for the schedule of upcoming matches. Tickets can be bought online, or at the entrance (but they may run out in advance for popular matches).

Brazil's Soccer Tournaments

January to May sees action between teams from the state of Rio de Janeiro, in the *Campeonato Carioca de Futebol* (the Carioca Soccer Championship). The best known state teams, all from the city of Rio, are Flamengo, Fluminense, Vasco and Botafogo: matches between any of these four are among the best on offer, as rivaly is so intense and passions so high.

Then, from May to December, the national championship, the *Brasileirão*, is fought out. In the *Brasileirão*, Rio's teams use the Maracanã as their home stadium, and you'll get to see teams from other parts of the country, such as Corin-thians from São Paulo and Grêmio from Porto Alegre.

1950 and 2014 World Cups

Maracanã was built in time to host the final of the 1950 World Cup. In the final of that year, when Brazil lost to Uruguay 2-1 (a national tragedy for Brazil, but a heroic achievement for Brazil's small southern neighbor), the attendance was just under 200,000 people. It was, and remained for many years, by far the world's largest stadium in terms of capacity. Crowds would be packed in, standing and sitting on long concrete rows, creating an electric atmosphere. By the time the 2014 World Cup came back to Brazil, Maracanã had been totally renovated (just in time) and its capacity reduced to just under 80,000, explained by the fact that individual seats replaced crowded standing areas (in accordance with FIFA standards).

Mário Filho

Since 1966, it has officially been called the Estádio Jornalista Mário Filho. It was renamed in honor of the early 20th-century sports journalist (a rarity in those days), who helped popularize soccer in Brazil, through newspaper articles. He was also involved in lobbying for the building of Maracanã stadium at its present site (the Maracanã neighborhood), when other locations were being considered. However, it's the original Maracanã name that has stuck.

As if helping to popularize soccer wasn't enough, Mário Filho is also

Live music at the Feira de São Cristóvão

co-credited with founding Rio's annual *desfile de escolas de samba* competition. Spanning several days during Carnaval, the colorful procession of samba schools is world-famous and a major draw to the *cidade maravilhosa*.

FEIRA DE SÃO CRISTÓVÃO

From the main gate of the Maracanã stadium, catch a 10-minute taxi (roughly US\$10) to the food stalls and live Brazilian music of the **Feira de São Cristóvão** ❸ (commonly known as the **Feira Nordestina**; www.feiradesaocristovao.org.br). It's open Tue–Thu 10am–6pm, and then stays open all weekend from Friday 10am to Sunday 9pm. For everyone to recover from the partying, it closes on Monday.

In the mid-20th century, large numbers of immigrants from Northeast Brazil came to Rio to escape the abject poverty and the periodic droughts which afflicted Brazil's most arid region. São Cristovão, near the port and long-distance bus terminal, became a meeting point for *Nordestinos* (northeasterners). It was here that an informal fair sprung up, with stalls selling typical food from the Northeast, along with parties featuring *forró*, the Northeastern country-style music.

Luiz Gonzaga

In 2003 the pavilion was renovated and renamed, becoming the 'Luiz Gonzaga Municipal Center of Northeastern Traditions'. Luiz Gonzaga (1912–89) is per-

haps the most famous musician from Northeast Brazil, thus the connection. The only thing is that having three names for one place is slightly confusing. Look on a map, and you'll probably see Feira de São Cristóvão (Saint Christopher's Fair). Speak to a local and they'll talk about the Feira Nordestina (Northeastern Fair). Taxi drivers should know all three versions.

Northeastern Food, Music and Art

Come in the weekdays for a quieter scene: this is a good time to shop and enjoy the restaurants without the crowds. Come at weekends for a place filled with energy and color, when there's live music everywhere: everything from *samba* to *forró* to *baião*, along with *axé* from Bahia and the Afro-Brazilian *maracatu*. There are capoeira dancers, comedy troupes and stalls selling *cachaça*, the Brazilian rum equivalent. It's also a place to stock up on arts and crafts: basketwork, ceramic figurines, wooden spoons and so on. In total, there are over 600 stalls, so there's of choice.

When it comes to typical Northeastern foods, you may want to try *tapioca* (manioc pancakes) and *aipim frito* (also called *macaxeira*, fried manioc root). There are also *escondidinhos de carne de sol* (a sort of shepherd's pie with sundried meat), *pamonha* (a dessert of sweet corn and coconut milk cooked in a corn husk) and much more.

Once you've taken in the atmosphere of the Feira Nordestina, the best way home is by taxi. A ride to Copacabana or Ipanema should cost around US\$15–20.

Soccer match on Icaraí Beach

NITERÓI

Catch a ferry across Guanabara Bay, to the city of Niterói on the other side, where you'll see modernist architecture by Niemeyer, a string of beaches, a fishing village and a fortress guarding the entrance of the bay. There are plenty of restaurants along the route for lunch or dinner.

DISTANCE: 12km (7 miles)
TIME: A full day
START: Niterói ferry terminal
END: Fortaleza de Santa Cruz, Niterói
POINTS TO NOTE: Personal ID is required on the visit to the fort at the end of the tour. Ferries to Niterói run on a regular basis daily, starting at 6am and ending at 11.30pm. During the weekly rush hour, they run every 10 minutes, and then every 20 minutes at other times. The route can be done entirely on foot, but we suggest a combination of walking with taxis and/ or buses. It can also be done by bike (which can be taken across on the ferry, but are hard to hire in Niterói).

Niterói, a city in its own right, but part of Greater Rio, encompasses the eastern shores of Guanabara Bay, plus a string of sandy beaches on the seaward side. It looks across the waters to its famous sister, Rio, the *cidade maravilhosa*. Thus *cariocas* (natives of Rio) joke that the best thing about Niterói is its view.

In response, residents of Niterói content themselves with the fact that their city regularly comes up in newspaper reports as one of the best places to live in Brazil. It's quieter and more down-to-earth than Rio, with plenty of opportunities for sailing, kayaking and surfing, plus good restaurants and less crowded beaches than Rio. Offering a good quality of life and a fast connection to Rio's Downtown by ferry, many *cariocas* have come to chose Niterói as their home. For visitors, Niterói has some unique attractions on offer and it makes an interesting, relaxing sort of day trip. And yes, just the view of Rio is worth the trip: all the famous peaks lined up in a remarkable silhouette.

PRAÇA QUINZE FERRY

Praça Quinze in Rio's Centro (Downtown) is the starting point of this journey. On the seaward side of this square, you'll see the busy ferry terminal. The easiest way to get here from any point in Rio is by taxi, although it's also a ten-minute walk from Cari-

Rio–Niteroi ferry

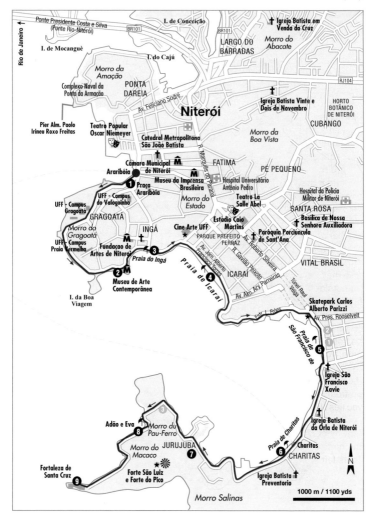

Oscar Niemeyer's Popular Theater of Niteroi

oca metro station. Note that there are a couple of options to Niterói, but for this route, you want to buy your tickets in the central section, where it is clearly marked 'Niterói'. This will take you to the Centro of Niterói, specifically Praça Araribóia square. Do not buy tickets and get on the catamaran marked 'Charitas' as that will take you to a different part of the city (but you may want to catch the Charitas ferry on the return to Rio).

During the weekly rush hour, the enormous *barcas* (ferries) are pretty packed, but they're frequent and you'll always get a seat. At weekends, the smaller and older ferries are used and it feels very leisurely. This older generation of ferries is from the 1960s and they have wooden benches and an outside deck that you can wander around.

As you cross over, you'll see the 13km (8-mile) -long Rio-Niterói bridge on your left. Behind this and on clear days, you can make out the *Dedo de Deus* (God's Finger) rock pinnacle in the Teresópolis mountains, which rise up from the back of the bay. Ahead of you lies Niterói's Downtown, backed by low rounded hills. Off to your right is the runway of Santos Dumont Airport and the cone-shaped Sugarloaf Mountain. To its left is the narrow mouth of Guanabara Bay. Guarding the other side are the battlements and white buildings of Santa Cruz Fort, your final stop on this route.

NITERÓI'S CENTRO

After 15 minutes (the total journey is 20), as you approach **Praça Araribóia ❶**, Niterói's central ferry terminal, look to your left on the waterfront. Curving forms painted in white were designed by Oscar Niemeyer, the renowned Brazilian modernist architect who was also responsible for designing most of Brasília's new government buildings, when the national capital moved there from Rio in 1960. Although built as a cultural complex, these Niemeyer structures in Niterói's Downtown have become a slight white elephant, being infrequently used and not easy to visit.

As you disembark, you walk through **Praça Araribóia**, a small open space before a busy road, the Avenida Visconde do Rio Branco. Named after the native tribal leader who helped the Portuguese defeat the French and expel them from Rio in 1567, Araribóia was granted lands on this side of the Bay. He's recognized as the founder of Niterói and his statue lies ahead of you. Notice across the road to your right the elegant Art Nouveau-style Post Office building, the **Palácio dos Correios**, built in 1914. Inside are temporary art exhibits by local artists. If you head over to see inside it, come back to the ferry terminal's taxi rank and ask for a ride to the Museu de Arte Contemporânea (or just say the 'MAC', pronounced 'Maki', the common name).

The journey will take you along the coast for 2km (1.2 miles), passing through **São Domingos**, a neighborhood with cobbled streets and the 17th-century **Gragoatá Fort**, guarding a narrow point of the bay, on the other side of which are the skyscrapers of Rio's Downtown.

MUSEU DE ARTE CONTEMPORÂNEA (MAC)

Soon after, you'll reach a flying saucer-shaped structure at the top of a hill overlooking the sea. This is the **Museu de Arte Contemporânea** ❷ (MAC) (Museum of Modern Art; Mirante da Boa Viagem; tel: 21-2602 2400; www.macniteroi.com.br; Tue–Sun 10am–6pm). This quintessential Oscar Niemeyer structure, with its modernistic concrete curves painted white, was built in 1996. It has become so iconic that it is now the emblem of Niterói. Inside, there are huge glass windows arranged as a band around the entire building, from which you can gaze down onto the sea and across the bay to the Sugarloaf. There are two levels, with art exhibits on show, but the building, not the art, is the main attraction.

Below the flying saucer, there are shallow pools of water and a panoramic view across Guanabara Bay, with the Sugarloaf in the background. In the foreground is the little white colonial-era church atop **Boa Viagem Island**, linked to the mainland by a pedestrian bridge. It has been closed for many years, but may reopen at some stage in the future, so keep an eye-out for signs of potential visits.

INGÁ & ICARAÍ BEACHES

Upon exiting the museum, turn right and walk down the hill. After 400 meters/yds you reach a tiny beach, **Praia do Ingá** ❸. Keep following the promenade and when you reach the end of the beach, there are a series of rocks, including the tall Pedra do Índio pinnacle, where you'll sometimes see surfers and mussel gatherers.

The next beach along is **Praia de Icaraí** ❹, backed by tall apartment buildings. This popular family spot has kiosks with piles of coconuts and cool coconut water to drink. On the beach, you'll see soccer, volleyball and *peteca* (volleyball using a shuttlecock) being played. Note the panoramic view of Rio, taking in all the major peaks, including the Sugarloaf, Corcovado, flat-topped Pedra da Gávea and Pico da Tijuca, the tallest of them all.

SÃO FRANCISCO

The next section is 9km (5.5 miles), so it is recommended to either catch a taxi or bus No. 33 to Jurujuba from one of the several bus stops along the beach. At the end of Icaraí, the road climbs up towards the right and then follows a series of curves around the Estrada

The futuristic Museu de Arte Contemporânea

Fróes headland, with mansions on either side, occasional glimpses of the bay on your right and a cycle track on your left.

You will then emerge onto the beachfront of **Praia de São Francisco** ❺, with low-rise buildings and a row of bars and restaurants on your left. If stopping off here, there are sandwich and ice-cream shops, as well as **Nói** ❶, a micro-brewery and bistro and **Mocellín** ❷, a steakhouse. On a low hill at the end of the beach is the quaint 17th-century **São Francisco de Xavier church**, with ancient mango trees and flamboyants providing red summer blossom.

CHARITAS

The next beach along is **Charitas** ❻, a 2km (1.2-mile) -long sandy stretch with kiosks for most of its length. This local gathering point draws crowds at weekends and in the summer for cold beers and *águas de coco* (coconut water) with *pastéis* (fried pasties filled with prawn, crab, meat or cheese). From under shady *amendoeira* trees, take in the lively local scene and enjoy Brazilian music (usually from a radio, but sometimes live).

Half way along you'll pass the small **Charitas ferry terminal**, with a covered pier (also designed by Niemeyer) heading over the water to the catamarans. These smaller, faster ferries (Mon–Fri 6.30am–8.30pm, every 15 minutes at peak hours, but only one per hour in the middle of the day) are a good option for your return to Rio. (There's a good café and bar on the water's edge if you find yourself with time to kill.) By the ferry terminal, also notice the shipping containers acting as storage units for windsurfing and Hawaiian canoeing clubs. In the water and on the sand are small and colorful fishing boats. Up the hill on your left is the Morro do Preventório favela and just beyond the ferry terminal on the beach is a sandy soccer pitch, popular with the local kids.

JURUJUBA

The bus or taxi will keep following the coast and as it curves around you'll enter **Jurujuba** ❼, a fishing village with mussel beds, sheltered bays filled with colorful fishing boats and hills covered in densely-packed houses. It's a low income area, slightly shabby and very informal. On the 29th June every year the village celebrates *São Pedro* (St Peter). A highlight is the sea procession of fishing boats, adorned in paper bunting, blasting out Brazilian music. As you reach the end of the village and drive over cobblestones, there's a small beach to your right. On your left are a couple of seafood restaurants, including **Berbigão** ❸. This is the final stop for the buses (which return regularly). Some buses continue on to Fortaleza Santa Cruz, in which case, stay on it. Otherwise, at the end of the little beach, walk up the hill with your back to the sea.

The fishing village of Jurujuba

Adam and Eve beaches

After 400 meters/yds you reach the top of the hill and it gradually descends. As it does, a view opens out in front of you: the Bay and Sugarloaf Mountain on the other side. There are two small beaches here, **Adão e Eva** ❽ (Adam and Eve). Keep following the road round the coast.

SANTA CRUZ FORT

At the end of the second beach you enter a military area and further up ahead you will be asked to present proof of ID. The road is cut into the rock above the sea and soon after you reach **Fortaleza de Santa Cruz** ❾, the fort which has been guarding the entrance to the Bay since 1555 (when it was originally founded by the French). Take time to walk around the grounds, with views out to sea and to the Sugarloaf which looms out of the sea, not far away. There are 45-minute tours of the ramparts (Tue–Sun, every half hour between 10am and 5pm), with tickets bought from a kiosk by the café.

To get back to the ferry to Rio, if not by taxi, walk back to the Jurujuba bus stop. All buses from here end go to the ferry terminal in Praça Arariboia, Niterói's Centro. During the week, a quicker return option is catching the Charitas ferry.

Food and Drink

❶ NÓI

Avenida Quintino Bocaiúva, 201, São Francisco; tel: 21-2611 0619; www.cervejarianoi.com.br; daily L and D. $$
This local microbrewery, whose name is an abbreviation of Niterói, offers a range of draft beers, from pale ales to chocolately stouts. On the menu is bistro-style food, including risottos, steaks and seafood. There are tables outdoors as well as in the modern light-filled dining room.

❷ MOCELLÍN

Avenida Quintino Bocaiúva, 151, São Francisco; tel: 21-3461 7080; www.origem dochurrasco.com; daily L and D. $$$
This contemporary *churrascaria* (steakhouse) has two sections: one for the all-you-can eat *rodízio* with a buffet, and another for à la carte dishes from the menu. The best seats are in the front, with a view towards Rio, across Guanabara Bay. Walking along the seafront, you'll find around 20 other bars and restaurants, one after the other.

❸ RESTAURANTE BERBIGÃO

Avenida Carlos Ermelindo Marins, 1275, Jurujuba; tel: 21-2714 4555; www.restauranteberbigao.com.br; daily L and D. $$
Set on the seafront overlooking a cobbled road and wooden fishing boats, the Berbigão has been serving Brazilian seafood dishes since the 1980s. Its decor is simple, the best tables are on the small veranda and the atmosphere is casual.

Horse-driven cart, Paquetá Island

PAQUETÁ ISLAND AND GUANABARA BAY

Take a ferry across the Bay of Guanabara to a flower-filled, vehicle-free island that has inspired novelists, poets and painters. Tour the island on foot, bike or horse-driven cart, passing old churches, little beaches and sights unique to the island.

DISTANCE: 5km (3 miles) on Paquetá, plus 32km (20 miles) ferry round-trip
TIME: A full day
START/END: Praça Quinze ferry terminal in Centro
POINTS TO NOTE: You need to head over in the morning to fit in the tour. Ferries depart at 1- to 3-hour intervals, depending on the time of day, with the first one leaving Rio at 5.30am and the last one returning from Paquetá at 11.10pm. There are additional services at the weekends and public holidays. Check the timetable and prices on www.grupoccr.com.br/barcas/linhas-horarios-tarifas. You can take bikes on the ferry for free, but places are limited to 10 bikes per ferry. The alternative is to hire a bike for the day upon arrival. Pick a clear day for this jaunt, but avoid sunny summer weekends when the island can become very crowded.

Towards the back of Guanabara Bay, sleepy Paquetá Island is a step back in time. There are no cars on the island's dirt roads, which are lined with colorful little houses and gardens. Its heritage is preserved for future generations as one of the state's cultural areas. The pace is sleepy, the crime rate negligible and the residents extremely friendly: this outing may provide a welcome break if the traffic and frantic activity of Rio become too much for you.

Eateries are unpretentious, serving typical Brazilian food and beers on little tables on the pavement. In the evenings, you'll hear live samba bands. There are lots of little beaches, but unfortunately, the sea is too polluted to swim in.

If you're entranced with Paquetá, it's easy to overnight here as there are some *pousadas* (rustic hotels) on the island. In any case, it's a lovely spot from which to watch the sunset (as is the ferry on the way back). While the sophisticated section of Rio society snootily turns its nose up at Paquetá, this is where local people go with their families for a fun and inexpensive day

Cart and horses at the ferryboat station on Paquetá Island

out, and it offers the visitor a unique experience outside the city. For those touring the island, it's shaped like a figure of 8, is roughly 2km (1.2 miles) long and at its narrowest point is only 100 meters/yds wide.

PRAÇA QUINZE DE NOVEMBRO

The easiest way to get to **Praça Quinze de Novembro** is by taxi. Otherwise, it's a 10-minute walk from Carioca metro station, and there are also many buses which stop on Rua Primeiro de Março (ask for Praça Quinze) on their way to Central (the main train terminal). Often shortened to Praça Quinze (Fifteen Square) and written Praça XV, the full name refers to the 15th November 1889, when Brazil was proclaimed a republic. This actually took place in the Praça da República, approximately 1km (0.6 miles) away, but there are many Fifteenth of November squares in Brazil. Should you find yourself waiting for a ferry, Route 6 (see page 55) also starts here and has details on sights in the Centro.

There are several ticket offices and points of departure lining the waterfront on Praça Quinze. Avoid the really busy section in the center as this is for the ferries to Niterói, across the bay (if you end up here by mistake, see Route 11, page 83, for a tour around for city). The Paquetá ticket booth is on the left as you look at the sea and is clearly marked. It's easy to get a ticket on the day.

The Ferry Trip

There are no numbered seats on the ferries, so take your pick. Upstairs is rowdy and fun, downstairs much quieter. The views are great from either deck, and you are free to wander around. The capacity is a staggering 2,000 passengers, minded by eight crew members. There are facilities, but don't expect anything fancy. Vendors of food, drink or souvenirs are forbidden, but they do occasionally creep on board to sell their wares.

As you pull away from the dock and the huge ferry does a U-turn, downtown Rio takes on quite a different perspective. To starboard is the runway of Santos Dumont airport, which services the Rio-São Paulo route. To the portside is the strange, green neo-Gothic building on Ilha Fiscal that hosted the last grand ball of the empire in 1889, shortly before the fall of the monarchy. Once you've rounded this, look back to see the Museu do Amanhã, the long white ultra-modern museum on Praça Mauá (see page 59). Across on the other side of the bay, you'll see the city of Niterói, with low rounded hills behind it. Further round is the mouth of the bay and Sugarloaf Mountain.

Some 20 minutes after departure from Praça Quinze, the ferry goes under the dramatic Rio-Niterói Bridge.

Pedal boats on the beach

At this stage you begin to appreciate why the first European visitors, 500 years ago, thought the bay was the mouth of a river, and therefore gave it the name River of January (the month they arrived). To port is the Ilha do Governador, home to the international airport, and beyond, the industrial areas.

On a clear day, you'll get a good view of the dramatic Serra dos Orgãos (Organ Mountain Range), which rise up from the back of the bay. Supposedly named for its resemblance to the pipes of an organ, though you would be forgiven for thinking the name is more anatomical in origin. Everywhere around you is evidence of Rio's rank as one of the world's busiest ports, with vessels in every stage of repair all over the bay.

PAQUETÁ ISLAND

Arrival on Paquetá

Arrival at the **Estação das Barcas ❶**, the Paquetá Ferry Terminal, is a noisy affair, as the crowd of local guides jostle for the most promising-looking visitors. Pick up some maps and leaflets at the tourist information booth straight ahead of you. By the ferry terminal, there are two bucolic squares. **Praça Pintor Pedro Bruno** has colorful bougainvilleas climbing up stone columns, while the shady **Praça Bom Jesus do Monte** hosted the first annual tree day in Brazil in 1904.

Horse-drawn Buggies

To get a feel for the place, hire a bike or start with a horse-drawn buggy ride (you will

Praia da Moreninha

notice a strong smell of horse when you disembark). You hire a buggy for either an hour or half an hour; prices are low, and regulated by the authorities. The trip may help you decide which beach you want to return to under your own steam, or where you want to spend a quiet interlude before returning to Rio.

The route taken on the buggy is bound to include an early stop at the **Cemitério dos Pássaros ②**. Possibly the only of its kind anywhere, this is a bird cemetery, which just goes to show you how attached the islanders are to their winged pets.

As you go along, you'll notice all around you well-kept gardens, with plants flourishing in this exhaust-free area. Striking flamboyant trees drip tangerine-colored flowers during the summer. Itineraries may vary slightly according to the condition of the unpaved roads, the whim of the buggy driver or even the mood of the horse.

Praia José Bonifácio

Then your driver will probably take you to the **Praia José Bonifácio ③**, the island 's busiest beach, with vendors of coconuts and snacks, and boats and canoes for hire. Facing west, it's a good point to watch the sunset. To your left as you face the water is the **Parque Darke de Mattos ④**, a park with ancient trees, walkways and panoramic views of the island and the bay from the Morro da Cruz viewpoint. The Jesuits established themselves here and from the hill, kaolin was extracted to produce porcelain crockery.

Praia da Moreninha

Boat moored off Paquetá

Onwards to **Praia da Moreninha ⑤**, the setting for the eponymous novel written by Joaquim Manuel de Macedo in the mid-18th century. From here you can climb to the top of the **Pedra da Moreninha ⑥**, via a wooden bridge, for outstanding views. The 1930s Normandy-style manor house on its own little island in front of you is the **Palácio de Brocoió**, one of the official residences of the Governor of Rio de Janeiro State.

Northern Beaches

Around the point you reach the tiny **Praia de São Roque ⑦**, much fre-

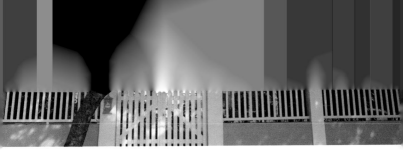

Colonial house

quented by fishermen. In the square behind the beach, the **Praça de São Roque**, is the local chapel, inaugurated in 1698. Here too is the **Poço de São Roque**, an old well with a stone top. The square is also home to the **Casa de Artes de Paquetá** ❶, a little cultural center and a good place for a coffee break.

The next beach is muddy **Praia do Lameirão** ❽, which is no good for swimming, but great for catching crabs. At the northernmost point of the island is **Praia de Catimbau** ❾, with splendid views of the Organ Mountain Range, and the distant mangrove swamps of Guapimirim in the distance.

Praia dos Tamoios

All roads lead eventually to **Praia dos Tamoios** ❿, named for the indigenous people who first lived here. This is a residential, as opposed to tourist, beach, but holds three points of interest for the visitor. Opposite house No. 425 is a rare and extremely old baobab tree, sacred in parts of Africa, with a circumference of 7 meters (23ft). The tree is protected by a preservation order, and known to local people as *Maria Gorda* (Fat Mary). In the middle of the road, opposite No. 341, is the last remaining cannon, which was used to hail the arrival of Pedro II, who visited Paquetá frequently in the early 1800s and used to call the place the 'Island of Love'. Also on this side of the island is the **Senhor Bom Jesus do Monte** is the island's parish

church, originally built in 1763 and with neo-Gothic interiors.

When you get back to the ferry terminal, this is where your buggy ride comes to an end. What you do with the rest of your time on the island depends on your tastes. A good option is to hire one of the various forms of bicycle available, return to a beach for a swim, and do some investigating on your own. For somewhere to eat, perhaps lunch or a beer by this stage, try **Bar da Tia Leleta** ❷.

Food and Drink

❶ **CASA DE ARTES DE PAQUETÁ**

Praça de São Roque, 31; tel: 21-3397 0517; www.casadeartes.org; daily L. $$

Inside a historic manor house which serves as a cultural center, featuring art and music, the Arte e Gula Café serves sandwiches, salads and *escondidinhos* (a local version of shepherd's pie). There's a little garden at the back and a building with Gaudí-inspired architectural features.

❷ **BAR DA TIA LELETA**

Rua Doutor Lacerda, 18, Praia dos Tamoios; tel: 21-3397 0656; Tue–Sun B, L and D. $$

Also known as Bar do Zarur, this simple little bar and restaurant serves coffees, cold beers, *pastéis* (savory pastries) and seafood lunches. A good place to chat to locals and enjoy live samba bands at the weekends.

DIRECTORY

Hand-picked hotels and restaurants to suit all budgets and tastes,
organised by area, plus select nightlife listings, an alphabetical
listing of practical information, a language guide and an overview
of the best books and films to give you a flavor of the city.

Accommodations	96
Restaurants	104
Nightlife	114
A–Z	116
Language	130
Books and Film	134

The Copacabana Palace

ACCOMMODATIONS

Most visitors to Rio make a beeline for those glimmering luxury hotels fronting Ipanema and Copacabana Beach, in the Zona Sul. But good deals can also be had just a block or two away from the water. A beach view may cost as much as 50 percent more than a room without one. There are good budget hotels in the suburbs of Glória, Flamengo and Botafogo and they can even be found in the aforementioned Copacabana and Ipanema.

Hostels of all stripes can be found in most neighborhoods, including Leblon, and there are some charming B&Bs and hotels in Santa Teresa worth checking out, such as Casa Cool Beans (see page 97). Santa Teresa offers a bohemian alternative to the hustle and bustle of the Zona Sul. This artistic neighborhood eschews dance clubs and street parties for quaint cafés and neighborhood bars. It's also a gastronomic hub, offering some of the finest off-the-beaten path dining in the city.

High season in Rio coincides with summer in the southern hemisphere, roughly from mid-December through Carnival (late February to mid-March). Advance reservations are necessary during high season, especially at Carnival and the New Year. Whatever time of year you travel to Rio, and as independent as you may be as a traveler, have at least your first night in Rio prebooked so you have a base to head for on arrival.

Centro

Windsor Guanabara Palace

Avenida Presidente Vargas, 392; tel: 21-2195 6000; www.windsorhoteis.com; metro: ML1, ML2 to Uruguaiana; bus: 369, 370; $$–$$$

One of Rio's most traditional downtown hotels (part of the Windsor group), and one of the largest, was completely refurbished in 2003 and is the best choice for travelers wanting to stay in the historic center away from the beach. The Guanabara Palace sits on Rio's widest avenue, opposite the Candelaria Church. Rooftop bar with a deck. Wheelchair access.

Flamengo/Lapa

Lapa Hostel

Rua do Resende, 43; tel: 21-2507 2869; www.lapahostelrio.com; metro ML1, ML2 at Cinelândia; 007, 010; $

Those who wish to live it up 24/7 in Lapa could do worse than this party

---

Prices for a standard double room for one night without breakfast in high season:

$$$$ = above $225
$$$ = $150–225
$$ = $75–150
$ = below $75

Copacabana Palace bathroom

hostel. About the only frills here seem to be the undersized pool table and the Nintendo Wii. Still, for travelers on a budget who don't mind the revelry, this is a solid option that is centrally located. Dorms only. Breakfast included.

Windsor Hotel Flórida

Rua Ferreira Viana, 81; tel: 21-2195 6800; www.windsorhoteis.com; metro: ML1, ML2 to Catete; bus: 151, 162, 170; $$

One of the older and more dependable budget establishments. Rooms have parquet floors and nice bathrooms. There's also a swimming pool. A block from Flamengo beach and next to the Metrô station, this hotel is very popular in high season.

Santa Teresa

Cama e Café

Rua Progresso 67; tel: 21-2225 4366; www.camaecafe.com.br; bus: 014; $–$$

The Cama e Café organization utilizes historic houses as bed-and-breakfast accommodation. It has around 200 houses on its books, many of which are located in upscale neighborhoods and possess amazing views. Soccer fanatics can stay near the Maracanã Stadium, while beach lovers can hang their hats mere steps from the sand in Copacabana or Ipanema. The focus is on providing the guest with an authentic Brazilian familial experience, and the local hosts range from teachers and chefs to photographers and jiu-jitsu instructors. 24-hour customer service.

Casa Cool Beans

Rua Laurinda Santos Lobo 136; tel: 21-2262 0552; www.casacoolbeans.com; bus: 006, 007, 014; $$

US expat owners David and Lance run an impeccable ship. The bright and tastefully decorated rooms all have air-conditioning, digital lockboxes, mini-refrigerators and the most comfortable mattresses outside of the Copacabana Palace Hotel. Wi-Fi here is lightning-fast, and a gourmet breakfast is included. There's a rooftop blue-tiled swimming pool and a terrace dining area offers great views of the surrounding mountains. Guests come away wowed by the high service standards. By far the best mid-range option in this peaceful Rio enclave.

Hotel Santa Teresa

Rua Alm. Alexandrino, 660; tel: 21-3380 0200; www.santa-teresa-hotel.com; bus: 006, 007, 014; $$$$

This lovely hotel, and its equally inviting lounge/bar, (see page 115) was the preferred base of Amy Winehouse when she played Rio. The celebrity endorsement isn't a surprise – this hotel's location in an expansive old manor is reminiscent of Hollywood's Chateau Marmont. However, the design here is 'tropical chic' and it is seen and felt everywhere, from the canopy beds to the terrace hammocks. The deckside pool and the view might be the biggest selling points of all.

Rooftop pool at the Hotel Rio Othon Palace

Copacabana/Leme

Hotel Atlântica Praia
Avenida Atlântica, 1456; tel: 21-2543 4123; www.atlanticopraia.com.br; bus: 318, 2018, 2115; $$

Once one of Rio's great hotels, and one of the world's first boutique hotels when it opened in 1950, the standards have somewhat slipped at the former Ouro Verde. The hotel remains intimate and refined, however; large rooms are tastefully decorated, many with nice balconies, and offer good value overall. Wheelchair access.

Belmond Copacabana Palace
Avenida Atlântica, 1702; tel: 21-2548 7070; www.belmond/copacabanapalace; Metro: ML1 at Cardeal Arcoverde; bus: 314, 354, 360; $$$$

Long the standard-bearer for luxury, the regal Copacabana Palace hasn't slipped, having been voted 'best hotel in the world' every year since 2012 by *World Travel* magazine. It has tastefully decorated rooms mixing classical and contemporary styles, great views, world-class spa services, an elegant pool and two excellent restaurants (see page 108). The suites are exceptional, and each one contains its own mini-wine cellar, among other amenities. All rooms have smart TVs and iPhone docks. Advance booking a must (at least six months for Carnival and New Years Eve). Wheelchair access.

Che Lagarto
Rua Barata Ribeiro, 111; tel: 21-3209 0348; www.chelagarto.com; metro: ML1 at Cardeal Arcoverde; bus: 127, 128, 314; $

On the opposite end of the spectrum from the Palace is this budget option. The lobby sets the tone for the entire place: it's hectic and the music is blasting, with masses of young backpackers milling about. It has 4-, 6-, 8-, 10- and 12-bed dorms, some with terraces. Small pool and rooftop bar. Not ideal for disabled travelers. Still, the staff is friendly, and a free buffet breakfast is included. Definitely a 'party' hostel.

Copa Hostel
Avenida Nossa Senhora de Copacabana, 1077; tel: 21-5521 2521; www.copahostel.com.br; bus: 119, 121, 123; $

This is another hostel option, located on the opposite end of Copacabana from Che Lagarto, but with a more mellow vibe. Situated one block from the beach, it offers 4-, 6- and 8-bed dorms, as well as a rooftop swimming pool. Free breakfast. They also rent apartments.

Excelsior
Avenida Atlântica, 1800; tel: 21-2195 5800; www.windsorhoteis.com; bus: 318, 2018, 2115, 2329; $$–$$$

An excellent option for anyone who can't afford the very top hotels. The location is superb, on the beachfront in the same block as the Copacabana Palace. Small rooftop pool.

Hotel Golden Tulip Regente
Avenida Atlântica; 3716; tel: 21-3545 5400;

Corner suite at the Porto Bay Rio Internacional

www.luxor-hotels.com; bus: 318, 2018, 2115; $$$

Overlooking the beach, near the Ipanema end of Copacabana, is this solid and reasonably priced luxury hotel. A bit labyrinthine, it has a business center, tiny pool and health club on the top floor. Service is very professional.

JW Marriott

Avenida Atlântica, 2600; tel: 21-2545 6500; www.marriott.com; bus: 318, 2018, 2115; $$$$

A modern hotel on the Copacabana beachfront offering exactly what clients, in particular business travelers, of this global chain expect. Small rooftop pool and excellent fitness center. It's worth paying extra for a beachfront room.

Miramar Hotel by Windsor

Avenida Atlântica, 3668; tel: 21-2195 6200; www.windsorhoteis.com; bus: 318, 2018, 2115; $$$$

Situated at the Ipanema end of Copa beach. Rooms have good views of the fort and docked fishing boats, and service is friendly. There's a glassed-in café/bar on the lobby floor, and a rooftop bar with a deck and swimming pool. Wheelchair access.

Pestana Rio Atlântica

Avenida Atlântica; 2964; tel: 21-2548 6332; www.pestana.com; bus: 318, 2018, 2115; $$$–$$$$

Modern 18-floor hotel, smack on Copacabana's beachfront avenue. This well-designed hotel, popular with both business travelers and families, has a Brazilian flavor. Half of the tiled rooms are suites and have balconies and Apple docking stations. The hotel has a rooftop pool, excellent health club, and even a small cinema. Wheelchair access.

Porto Bay Rio Internacional

Avenida Atlântica; 1500; tel: 21-2546 8000; www.riointernacional.com.br; bus: 318, 2018, 2115; $$$–$$$$

The polished Internacional is popular with business travelers and vacationers. The business center is one of the city's best. The elegant rooms are spacious and have great balconies and beach views. Rooftop pool, fitness center and restaurant.

Hotel Rio Othon Palace

Avenida Atlântica, 3264; tel: 21-2106 1500; www.othon.com.br; bus: 318, 2018, 2115; $$$

This high-rise, hugely popular with tour groups, seems to have been around forever. Rooms are tastefully decorated, and the hotel has a rooftop pool and a fine gym. Wheelchair access. Its sister hotels include the Savoy Othon, located a couple blocks from the beach and the Aeroporto Othon downtown. These hotels are of varying degrees of sophistication, and the two closest to the beach are ideal for watching the New Year celebrations.

Sofitel Rio

Avenida Atlântica, 4240; tel: 21-2525 1232; www.sofitel.com; metro: ML1 at General

Pool at the Hotel Caesar Park

Osório; bus: 360, 382, 557; $$$$

Opened by Frank Sinatra in 1979, this classic luxury hotel has a superb location at the end of Copacabana closest to Ipanema, across from the fort; the views over the whole sweep of Copacabana are nothing short of spectacular. There are two pools. The restaurant, Le Pré Catelan (see page 108), is one of Rio's best, and one of only a handful of Michelin-starred establishments in the city. Wheelchair access.

Windsor Atlantica Hotel

Avenida Atlântica, 1020; tel: 21-3873 8888; www.windsorhoteis.com.br; $$$$

This landmark hotel, ideally located at the closest point of Copacabana to the city center, is one of Rio's largest and best. There are two pools, a spa and a fitness center. Good for business or leisure.

Ipanema/Leblon

Hotel Caesar Park

Avenida Vieira Souto, 460; tel: 21-2525 2525; www.sofitel.com; metro: ML1 at General Osório; bus: 314, 318, 360; $$$$

This top-flight, luxury hotel is a favorite of business travelers and the likes of the Japanese, Spanish and Swedish royal families. The 45-sq-meter (488-sq-ft) Imperial Suite is one of Rio's best. Rooms are elegant and ample, service excellent. Private security watches over guests on the beach and there is also a small rooftop pool. Breakfast on the top floor overlooking Ipanema and Corcovado, is a standout. Wheelchair access.

Everest Rio Hotel

Rua Prudente de Morais, 1117; tel: 0800-600 0995; www.everest.com.br; bus: 177, 314, 318, 360; $$–$$$

The location is excellent: just a block from the beach behind Caesar Park, it's surrounded by Ipanema's restaurants, bars and boutiques. Rooms feature large windows; the views from the rooftop deck and the Grill 360° Restaurant take in Corcovado. Though popular with business travelers, there is a play area well suited for families. Nearby, on Rua Maria Quitéria, is the Everest Park Hotel, a less expensive member of the same chain.

Fasano

Avenida Vieira Souto, 80; tel: 21-3202 4000; www.fasano.com.br; bus: 318, 360, 382; $$$–$$$$

Rio's most stylish and sophisticated boutique hotel offers an eclectic mix of tastes and styles. Located at the Copacabana end of Ipanema beach, Fasano's bar (Baretto-Londra) and Italian seafood restaurant (Fasano Al Mare) are two of Rio's most sought-after spots. The rooftop deck and pool, with fabulous views over Ipanema, are for guests only.

Ipanema Plaza

Rua Farme de Amoedo 34; tel: 21-3687 2000; www.ipanemaplaza.com.br; metro: ML1 at General Osório; bus: 413, 426, 435; $$$–$$$$

Located one block back from Ipanema beach, this hotel is a favorite with travelers preferring tranquil and sophisticated

Room at Fasano

Ipanema to Copacabana. Stylish and modern with a rooftop pool. Wheelchair access.

Leblon Spot Design Hostel

Rua Dias Ferriera, 636; tel: 21-2137 4310; www.leblonspot.com; bus: 173, 438, 439; $–$$

Tranquil and inviting, this hostel is situated in a quiet enclave adjacent to a fantastic French chop house, CT Boucherie. It offers 4-, 6-, 8-, 10- and 12-bed dorms, plus 5 suites (two with street views) and two privates with shared bathroom located in the adjacent building. Spot Design's cozy, spotless environment, as well as the professional service, are hallmarks of a hotel, but the communal spirit is pure hostel. Can arrange pub crawls and parties.

Marina All Suites

Avenida Delfim Moreira, 696; tel: 21-2172 1100; www.marinaallsuites.com.br; bus: 124, 132, 157; $$$–$$$$

The finest hotel on the Leblon end of the beach. Rooms, as the name suggests, are suites and the top nine have been decorated by celebrated Brazilian designers, making this one of the city's few boutique hotels. The 360-degree views from the rooftop pool are excellent (Gávea mountain is very close). The bistro restaurant, with ocean views, is recommended. Close by is the more traditional Marina Palace Hotel (www.hotelmarina.com.br), which is another fine option.

Praia Ipanema & Best Western Plus Sol Ipanema

Avenida Vieira Souto, 706/320; tel: 21-2540 4949 (Praia), 21-2525 2020 (Sol); www.praiaipanema.com.br, www.solipanema.com; bus (Praia and Sol) 177, 314, 318; $$$

These unremarkable hotels' location on Ipanema beach, only shared by the much more expensive Caesar Park and Fasano, makes them excellent value. Also close to many of the best restaurants and bars in Ipanema.

Vidigal/São Conrado

Royal Tulip Rio

Avenida Aquarela do Brasil, 75; tel: 21-3323 2200; www.royaltulipriodejaneiro.com; bus: 177, 360, 382; $$–$$$

In São Conrado, bordered by the beach, the Gávea Golf Club and the Fashion Mall, the Royal Tulip (formerly the Inter-Continental but now under the Golden Tulip banner) is a true resort hotel, or as much of a resort as you can get in a metropolitan city. Popular with American groups, it has tennis courts, multiple swimming pools and good restaurants. It is also well located for events at Riocentro and for business travelers working with businesses located in Barra.

Sheraton Rio Hotel & Towers

Avenida Niemeyer, 121, tel: 21-2274 1122; www.sheraton-rio.com; bus: 177, 360, 382; $$$$

Be prepared to flex your wallet – this is the only hotel directly on a beach. A first-

rate luxury resort, it has tennis courts, two pools, a great gym, two bars and five (yes, *five*) restaurants, four with ocean views. Perfect for relaxed privacy, but still close to Leblon's restaurants and clubs. Sheraton guards patrol the beach regularly. 'Tower' apartments are excellent. Wheelchair access.

Barra da Tijuca

Sheraton Barra Hotel & Suites

Avenida Lúcio Costa, 3150; tel: 21-3139 8000; www.sheraton-barra.com.br; bus: 302, 309, 316; $$$–$$$$

Reflecting the growing importance of Barra da Tijuca, a number of serious hotels have sprung up along the beachfront to cater mainly for South Americans who want to be in the heart of 'new' Rio. Leading the pack is the Sheraton Barra Hotel & Suites, a five-star property offering well-equipped rooms and suites all with ocean views and balconies. The hotel has a good pool area, spa and fitness facilities, and sits right in front of Barra beach. Closest of the major hotels to Riocentro, the city's main convention and conference center. Wheelchair access.

Angra dos Reis

Hotel Vila Galé Eco Resort

Estrada Benedito Adelino, 8413; tel: 24-3379 2800; www.villagale.com; $$$$

This property 160km (100 miles) from Rio, is ideal for those travelers looking for a full resort experience close to Rio. It has the facilities you might expect of a top resort, such as a sprawling pool and three restaurants, but with a focus on sustainable environmental practices. Located on its own beach with views of Angra Bay, in a preserved area of Atlantic rainforest, it offers excellent walks and treks.

Pestana Angra

Estrada Benedito Adelino, 3700; tel: 24-3364 2005; www.pestana.com; $$$$

Luxurious and romantic getaway close to Angra, with 27 individual bungalows strategically placed in the grounds around a central pool, restaurant and bar complex. Memorable views across Angra Bay to the Atlantic rainforest.

Paraty

Pousada do Ouro

Rua Dr Pereira, 145; tel: 24-3371 4300; www.pousadaouro.com.br; $$

This handsome *pousada* in Paraty's historic center was used in the 1983 film *Gabriela*. It has attractive rooms, safes, saunas, a spa and bar, and a smart common area. Breakfast included.

Pousada Porto Imperial

Rua Tenente Francisco Antônio; tel: 24-3371 2323; www.pousadaportoimperial.com.br; $$$

One of the largest *pousadas* in the historic center (near the river, behind the Igreja dos Remédios), this property is over 200 years old and has more facilities than any other lodging in Paraty. Its attractive rooms are all named after famous women; there's a pool, tennis court, and a lovely patio and gardens. Breakfast included.

Fazenda Ponte Alta

Búzios

Byblos

Morro do Humaitá, 14; tel: 22-2623 1162; www.pousadabyblos.com.br; $$–$$$
One of the original *pousadas* in the area, Byblos maintains high standards. It sits on a hill overlooking Armação and Ossos beaches and is a 5-minute walk from Rua das Pedras. Decktop pool. Breakfast included.

Casas Brancas

Morro do Humaitá, 10; tel: 22-2623 1458; www.casasbrancas.com.br; $$$–$$$$
Not only one of the most picturesque *pousadas* in Búzios, but also one of the most luxurious. Popular with travelers looking for something special. Excellent service. Decktop pool.

Hibiscus Beach

Rua 1 No. 22; tel: 22-2623-6221; www.hibiscusbeach.com.br; $$–$$$
Hibiscus Beach consists of individual bungalows and is located above João Fernandes beach. It has its own swimming pool nestled in a peaceful, tropical garden. Good for families or couples. Unusually, it is British owned and managed, yet retains a distinctly Búzios charm.

Pousada do Martin Pescador

Enseada do Gancho, 15A; tel: 22-2623 1449; www.martinpescador.com.br; $$
Beautifully situated, this *pousada* hugs the hills above Manguinhos beach. Beds are elevated so that the view from one's pillow is of the bay. There's a congenial common area and a squash court and pool area. The sauna comes with a view of the sea. Breakfast is included.

Le Relais La Borie

Geriba Beach; tel: 22-2620 8504; www.la borie.com.br; $$$$
This delightful *pousada*, located directly on Geriba beach, is one of the largest and best equipped on the Búzios peninsula. Restaurant, two bars, two pools and an indoor jacuzzi.

Vale do Paraíba

Fazenda Arvoredo

Estrada Santa Maria, 68, Barra do Piraí, RJ; tel: 24-2447 2001; www.hotelarvoredo.com.br; $$$–$$$$
This large and lovely former coffee plantation dates from the middle of the 19th century. The immaculate rooms, all identical, are located in former slaves' quarters. Situated on 1,140 acres (460 hectares), with opportunities for hiking, biking and horse-riding. The farm also has a large pond for rowing boats, and a rustic pool. Meals included.

Fazenda Ponte Alta

Parque Santana, Barra do Piraí, RJ; tel: 24-2443 5159, www.pontealta.com.br; $$–$$$
This beautiful coffee estate is perfect if you want to immerse yourself in Brazilian history. Each of the nine rooms is different; some are in the main house, others across the garden in former slaves' quarters (*senzala*). Swimming pool. All meals included.

Moqueca (fish stew)

RESTAURANTS

As one would expect from a beachside city in the tropics, the dining scene in Rio is, on the whole, very casual. It has an interesting mix of cuisines, but can't compare to somewhere like Sydney or San Francisco in terms of diversity. Below are the some of the main types you'll encounter.

At the most basic level are the *quiosques*, the beach kiosks mainly selling *água de coco* (coconut water) and beers. Next up, and found everywhere, are *lanchonetes*, the traditional and simply-decorated snack bars. Most sell fried and baked pastries and a wide range of *sucos naturais*, fresh fruit juices. The larger *lanchonetes* quite often have a *padaria* (bakery) and *mercearia* (grocery) attached to them and also serve *pratos do dia* (lunch of the day).

A *boteco* or *botequim* is a sort of *carioca* pub, combining *chopes* (draft beers) with Brazilian food like *bolinhos de bacalhau* (cod fritters) and *feijoada* (black bean stew). They're generally lively, crowded and have live music at weekends. At lunchtime, many casual restaurants work on a *comida a quilo* basis (buffet food paid by the weight). *Churrascarias* are steakhouses, either working on a *rodízio* basis (all-you-can-eat meats with a buffet of salads) or à la carte (from a menu). A variation on this is a *galeteria*, specializing in barbecued chicken served at a bar counter.

Regional influences include *comida mineira*, food from Minas Gerais state, which is rustic and hearty. You'll also find German food, a multitude of pizzarias, traditional Arab dishes and laid-back Brazilian sushi bars. Peruvian, Mexican and vegetarian places are growing in popularity, as are artisan beer bars.

In the historic heart of Rio (like the Centro, Santa Teresa and Botafogo), terraced houses turned into restaurants have an old-world bohemian charm. High-end restaurants serving contemporary dishes can be found in the international hotel chains and dotted around the Zona Sul.

Prices for a two-course meal with a drink:
$$$$ = above $50
$$$ = $30–50
$$ = $15–30
$ = below $15

Barra da Tijuca

Bar do Oswaldo

Estrada do Joá, 3896; tel: 21-2493 1840; www.bardooswaldo.com.br; daily L and D. $

Established in 1946 and famous for its sweet *batida* drinks, this casual

Copacabana restaurant   *Frango com quiabo (chicken with okra)*

boteco has outdoor tables and also serves Brazilian favorites, like steaks and *feijoada*.

La Botticella

Estrada Sorima, 347; tel: 21-2495 9340; www.labotticella.com.br; Tue–Sat D, Sun L and D. $$

Homemade pastas, pizzas and Argentinian dishes are the order of the day here, along with a good selection of wines, are served in a rustic Italian cantina setting.

Hansl

Rua Professor Júlio Lohman, 132, Joá; tel: 21-2493 0279; www.hansl.com.br; Estrada; Mon–Fri D, Sat–Sun L and D. $$

Various types of fondues, plus an array of Germanic dishes, are on offer in a cozy chalet-like setting. From its hillside location, there are panoramic views over tropical forests to the beaches and buildings of Barra.

Laguna

Ilha da Gigóia; tel: 21-2495 1229; www.restaurantelaguna.com.br; Thu–Fri D, Sat–Sun L and D. $$$

Reservations are required for this candle-lit seafood restaurant on Ilha da Gigóia. Set within tropical gardens on this island in the middle of a lagoon, the only way to get there is by catching a little passenger boat from Barra Point. Around the island are a couple of more casual options, also accessible by boat.

Nativo

Avenida Lúcio Costa, 1976; tel: 21-2486 3949; www.nativobarrestaurante.com.br; daily L and D. $$

On the seafront and with outdoor tables, this casual and comfy eatery serves family favorites, like steaks, pizzas and salads. You can also order *acarajé* (bean fritter stuffed with a spicy paste), from the *Baianas* (women dressed in traditional Bahian dresses) on the street corner.

Pe'ahi

Avenida do Pepê; tel: 21-2492 1286; daily L and D. $

Just behind a popular surfing and kitesurfing spot on Barra beach, this chilled out sushi bar is named after the famous Hawaiian surf spot. As you eat your sashimi, you can watch surf videos, then amble into the surf shop.

Botafogo

Fogo de Chão

Avenida Repórter Néstor Moreira; tel: 21-2279 7117; www.fogodechao.com.br; daily L and D. $$$

Part of a chain of *churrascarias* in Brazil and the US, this branch has a view of Botafogo Bay and the Sugarloaf (walk out onto the terrace). By the front door, you'll see racks of beef ribs (the house specialty) roasting over hot embers. The decor is modern and elegant and the waiters are very attentive. Reservations are advisable for dinner and at weekends.

Bar Brasil

Irajá

Rua Conde de Irajá, 109; tel: 21-2246 1395; www.irajagastro.com.br; daily L and D. $$$

The emphasis is on contemporary Brazilian cuisine, where traditional dishes are given a creative touch by skilled chefs. The restaurant is set within a renovated historic house, where plants growing in a vertical garden take up one of the walls. Reservations recommended for dinner and weekends.

Centro

Amarelinho

Praça Floriano, 55; tel: 21-2240 8434; www.amarelinhocinelandia.com.br; daily L and D. $

A traditional *choperia* (beer bar and restaurant) serving *chopes* (draft beers), with *pastéis* (fried savory pastries, filled with cheese or minced meat), steaks and hearty *feijoada*. Founded in 1921, it's one of Rio's more traditional spots. It's nothing fancy, but very typical, where city workers congregate around tables on the square for lunch and happy hours.

Atrium

Praça Quinze de Novembro, 48; tel: 21-2220 0193; www.restauranteartium.com.br; Mon–Fri L. $$

Set within the 18th-century Paço Imperial (Imperial Palace), contemporary Brazilian dishes are served in a historic dining room, with stone walls, classic furnishings and oil paintings.

Bar Brasil

Avenida Mem de Sá, 90, Lapa; tel: 21-2509 5943; Mon–Sat L and D. $$

Part of Rio's cultural heritage, and founded in 1907 by Austrians, this traditional neighborhood bar and restaurant feels like a step back in time. Germanic dishes, like pork cutlets, sausages and sauerkraut are served with cold beers in unfussy surrounds.

Bar Luiz

Rua da Carioca, 39; tel: 21-2262 6900; www.barluiz.com.br; Mon and Sat L, Tue–Fri L and D. $$

One of the city's oldest surviving establishments, this *botequim* has hosted a long roster of illustrious *cariocas*. Founded in 1887, it moved to its present location near the Largo da Carioca in 1927. The dining room has simple tables, white tablecloths and photos of old Rio. The menu is German.

Cais do Oriente

Rua Visconde de Itaboraí, 8; tel: 21-2233 2531; www.caisgourmet.com.br; daily L and D. $$$

Located in a listed warehouse built in 1878, with bar brick walls and close to the docks and city center, this large establishment is spread over three floors and offers a mix of atmospheres and cuisines where East meets West and Brazil meets the Orient.

Cedro do Líbano

Rua Senhor dos Passos, 231; tel: 21-2224

Confeitaria Colombo

0163; www.cedrodolibano.com.br; Mon–Sat L. $$

Brazilian cuisine has a strong Arab influence, as a result of Lebanese and Syrian immigration in the early 20th century. The 'Cedar of Lebanon', founded in 1948, is one of Rio's more traditional Arab restaurants. On the menu are homemade classics from hummous to grilled lamb and sweet pastries.

Confeitaria Colombo

Rua Gonçalves Dias, 32; tel: 21-2505 1500; www.confeitariacolombo.com.br; Mon–Sat B and L. $$

Founded in 1894, this is Rio's most famous café. In a traditional Belle Époque setting, with large mirrors from Antwerp, intricate woodwork and marble surfaces, it serves breakfast, a buffet lunch, plus sweet pastries and salty snacks into the early evening (until 8pm weekdays or 5pm Saturdays), when office workers go home.

Hachiko

Travessa do Paço, 10; tel: 21-2533 6366; www.restaurantehachiko.com.br; Mon–Sat L and D. $$$

A hidden doorway leads upstairs to a Japanese restaurant on the second floor of a renovated manor house. Apart from traditional sushi choices, this spot is known for its *menu de degustação*, where the focus is on multiple small courses, each one a surprise.

Rio Minho

Rua do Ouvidor, 10; tel: 21-2509 2338; Mon–Fri L. $$$

This is one of Rio's oldest restaurants, founded in 1884 and set within a historic *azulejo* tile-covered building. Seafood dishes are the specialty, which include classic recipes from France and Brazil. There are tables on the pavement – a good spot for a relaxed beer.

Copacabana and Leme

Azumi

Rua Ministro Viveiros de Castro, 127, Copacabana; tel: 21-2541 4294; daily L and D. $$$

One of the few truly authentic Japanese restaurants in Rio, Azumi has been running since 1989. The decor is simple, with cozy seating areas, including private *tatame* rooms and stools around the sushi bar. The menu has an immense choice, from well-known sashimis to cooked delicacies which few people outside Japan would have tried.

Brasileirinho

Avenida Atlântica, 3564, Copacabana; tel: 21-2267 3148; www.cozinhatipica.com.br; daily L and D. $$

As the name suggests, the 'Little Brazilian' serves regional food from Brazil, including steaks, seafood and *feijoada*. The restaurant, filled with wicker lanterns and all sorts of other craftwork, has a casual and contemporary feel.

Restaurant in Ipanema

Cipriani

Avenida Atlântica, 1702, Copacabana; tel: 21-2548 7070; www.belmond.com; daily L and D. $$$$

This elegant restaurant in the Copacabana Palace Hotel overlooks the cinematic pool, which, illuminated at night, evokes the glamour of the 1920s. The focus is on northern Italian cuisine with contemporary touches. There's a good wine list and the decor is plush. Reservations are recommended.

Marius Degustare

Avenida Atlântica, 290, Leme; tel: 21-2104 9000; www.marius.com.br/2012; daily L and D. $$$$

In Leme, overlooking the beach, this high-class *churrascaria* also serves lobster and a whole array of seafood and has a salad bar with vegetables from a private garden. What makes this place most unique is its decoration – with walls covered in shells, fishing nets and memorabilia, it feels like you're in a mysterious underwater cavern.

O Caranguejo

Rua Barata Ribeiro, 771, Copacabana; tel: 21-2235 1249; www.restauranteocaranguejo.com.br; daily L and D. $$

Translated as 'The Crab', this traditional *carioca*-style restaurant and bar focuses on seafood. Classic *petiscos* (snacks), popular after a day on the beach, include the *pastel de cama-rão* (shrimp pastry) and *casquinha de siri* (stuffed crab shell), which can also be ordered at the pavement bar. Main dishes include octopus, squid, grilled sardines and *moqueca* stews.

Le Pré Catelan

Avenida Atlântica, 4240, Copacabana; tel: 21-2525 1160; www.gastronomiasofitel. com.br; Mon–Sat D. $$$$

Located in the Sofitel Rio Hotel, this high-end French restaurant offers nouveau cuisine in an elegant dining space with panoramic views along the entire stretch of Copacabana Beach as far as the Sugarloaf Mountain. On the menu are carefully crafted small portions combining French techniques with exotic flavors from Brazil's tropical coastline and Amazon rainforest. Reservations are recommended.

Flamengo

Café Lamas

Rua Marquês de Abrantes, 18; tel: 21-2556 0799; www.cafelamas.com.br; daily L and D. $$

One of the oldest restaurants in Rio, Café Lamas has served people like President Getúlio Vargas and the celebrated writer Machado de Assis. Founded in 1874, its has simple decor and a traditional menu focused on steaks.

Intihuasi

Rua Barão do Flamengo, 35; tel: 21-2225 7653; www.intihuasi.art.br; Tue–Sat L and

Cipriani at Copacabana Palace

D, Sun L. $$

Classic Peruvian dishes like ceviche (marinated fish) and a wide range of typical meat, potato and corn options are prepared by a Peruvian chef in a cozy and colorful setting.

Rotisseria Sirio Libanesa

Largo do Machafo, 29; tel: 21-2205 2047; Mon–Sat B, L and D. $

This simply-decorated *lanchonete* specializes in savory Arab snacks, like *kibes* and *esfirras*, as well as meals including grilled meat kebabs with lentils and stuffed cabbage leaves.

Tacacá do Norte

Rua Barão do Flamengo, 35; tel: 21-2205 7545; daily B, L and D. $

If you're wanting to try authentic food from the Amazon region, this is a good bet. It's a very simple snack bar, serving fruit juices and ice creams made from Amazonian fruit, plus açaí served the natural way (unsweetened). For something to eat, try the soups: *tacacá* and *caldo de tucupi*, both of which are foods of Amazon tribes and probably quite different from anything you've ever tried.

Ipanema

Casa da Feijoada

Rua Prudente de Morais, 10; tel: 21-2247 2776; www.cozinhatipica.com.br; daily L and D. $$

The slogan – and reality – at this restaurant is 'Every day is a day for *feijoada*'. This long-standing, small and simple restaurant is right next to the Ipanema square that hosts the *Feira Hippie* (Hippie Fair) in Ipanema every Sunday. The national dish, *feijoada*, is a must, where you'll get hearty black bean stew accompanied by side dishes like *farofa* (toasted manioc root meal) *couve* (kale) and rice. The menu also includes other classic Brazilian dishes, such as *moqueca*.

Fasano al Mare

Avenida Vieira Souto, 80; tel: 21-3202 4000; www.fasano.com.br; daily L and D. $$$$

Stylish Italian seafood restaurant located in the Fasano Hotel on the Ipanema beachfront. Like its sister restaurant, Gero, Fasano Al Mare is one of the most sought-after eateries for the city's in-crowd. Not cheap, but an experience in good living. Menu items include tuna carpaccio, *bacalhau* (salt cod) and tiramisu, along with a good wine list.

Gero

Rua Anibal de Mendonça, 157; tel: 21-2239 8158; www.fasano.com.br; daily L and D. $$$$

Gero is one of the hotspots on Rio's gastronomic map, popular with those who matter in artistic, financial and political circles. Part of the Fasano family that also owns and runs the hotel in Ipanema. Its sophisticated Italian menu offers an interesting mix

Juice bar in Ipanema

of classical and innovative dishes. A treat for business or pleasure, but reservations are a must. There is also a branch in Barra da Tijuca at 190 Avenida Erico Verissimo.

Gula Gula

Rua Henrique Dumont, 57; tel: 21-2259 3084; www.gulagula.com.br; daily L and D. $$

The Gula Gula restaurants are a chain of relaxed, but fashionable, *carioca* eateries in Rio, serving salads, grilled meats and pastas. The best known is perhaps the Ipanema branch, located just one block back from the beach. It offers excellent value for money given the quality of setting, cuisine and service.

Manoel & Juaquim

Rua Barão da Torre, 162; tel: 21-2522 1863; www.manoelejuaquim.com.br; daily L and D. $$

A lively and informal chain of *botequims* where *chopes* (draft beers) are served with *petiscos* (appetizers), like crab pastries. The decoration is that of a traditional *carioca* bar, with traditional Portuguese influences.

New Natural

Rua Barão da Torre, 173; tel: 21-2247 9363; daily B, L and D. $$

A pioneer in vegetarian and organic food in Rio, the New Natural is set within a two-story brick house. At lunchtime there is a varied buffet with salads,

sushi and more. The property also has a natural foods shop.

Satyricon

Rua Barão da Torre, 192; tel: 21-2521 0627; www.satyricon.com.br; daily L and D. $$$$

The fine Italian menu emphasises fresh seafood. A favorite of stars and business magnates, it features a sushi bar and an attention-getting dining room. Originally founded in Búzios in the 1980s, it's been one of Rio's most sought-after high-end restaurants for over 25 years.

Jardim Botânico

Bráz

Rua Maria Angélica, 129; tel: 21-2525 0687; www.casabraz.com.br; daily L and D. $$

With the atmosphere of a typical 1920s Italian cantina, Bráz is one of Rio's leading pizza houses, considered by many to serve the city's best artisan pizzas. It's very popular, so expect to have to wait in line.

Couveflor

Rua Pacheco Leão, 724; tel: 21-2512 6054; www.couveflor.com.br; daily L. $

From salads to hot dishes, a wide range of lunch options are available at the self-serve buffet counter. This informal eatery is set within an old manor house in the charming area of Horto, around the corner from the Botanic Garden.

At Palaphita Kitch

Filé de Ouro
Rua Jardim Botânico, 731; tel: 21-2259 2396; Tue–Sun L and D. $$
Running since the 1960s, this is one of Rio's most traditional *churrascarias*, where the specialty is 300g steaks served with typical Brazilian accompaniments, like *farofa* (toasted manioc root meal). It's small inside and expect a line outside at weekends.

Olympe
Rua Custódio Serrão, 62; tel: 21-2539 4542. Mon–Sat D; Fri L and D. $$$$
From one of France's most traditional gastronomic families, Claude Troisgros and his son Thomas combine French and Brazilian influences in a cozy sophisticated setting. Reservations are a must.

Lagoa

Bar Lagoa
Avenida Epitácio Pessoa, 1674; tel: 21-2523 1135; www.barlagoa.com.br; daily L and D. $$
This charming 1934 *botequim* has an Art Deco interior and a veranda facing the lagoon. It's great for lunch or dinner, but late in the evening is when things really get going – and noisy. The fare is German, and includes classics such as *Kassler Rippchen* (ribs) *mit Sauerkraut*, and *bratwurst* sausages with potato salad, backed by international favorites. Portions are large.

Ki
Rua Fonte da Saudade, 179; tel: 21-2535 3848; www.restauranteki.com.br; daily D. $$$
Gourmet Japanese cuisine, with contemporary touches, plus a wide selection of sakes, are served in a romantic and softly-lit setting of a renovated manor house.

Palaphita Kitch
Avenida Epitácio Pessoa (Kiosk 20, Parque do Cantagalo); tel: 21-2227 0837, daily D. $$
The lagoon-side kiosks along the shores of the Lagoa are great for alfresco food and drinks. This trendy version, open in the evenings for cocktails and casual bar bites, has a rustic Amazon-inspired setting.

Leblon

Antiquarius
Rua Aristides Espinola, 19; tel: 21-2294 1049; www.antiquarius.com.br; daily L and D. $$$$
This small and elegant spot has been serving exquisitely prepared classic Portuguese and Brazilian dishes since 1977. The clientele can be gauged by the Mercedes and BMWs with bored drivers waiting outside. The ambiance, though, is unpretentious. Upstairs, antiques are for sale, hence the name.

Bracarense
Rua José Linhares, 85; tel: 21-2294 3549; daily B, L and D. $

A typical local restaurant selling sandwiches and juices

A traditional *botequim*, the Bracarense is a casual gathering spot with tables on the pavement, where locals drop by throughout the day. From a coffee in the morning, to a steak for lunch and beers with codfish fritters in the evenings, it's a reliable little place.

This tiny *botequim* has been running for over a century, and it's a favorite among locals. Along with beers, specialties include *caldinho de feijão* (black bean broth), fried sardines and pork crackling. When there's a soccer match on TV, be prepared for a true Brazilian experience.

Celeiro

Rua Dias Ferreira, 199; tel: 21-2274 7843; www.celeiroculinaria.com.br; Mon–Sat L and D. $$

This attractive restaurant on Leblon's major restaurant row serves *comida a quilo*, a place where you pay by weight (in this case, a high-end version). The simple, light fare includes salads, sandwiches and quiches; the salad bar will delight vegetarians and non-veggies alike. The outdoor tables are popular with young people.

Giuseppe Grill

Avenida Bartolomeu Mitre, 370; tel: 21-2249 3055, www.bestfork.com.br; daily L and D. $$$$

Arguably Rio's most stylish and sophisticated steakhouse, this place also serves fresh seafood and a range of premium wines. The original Giuseppe Grill, located in the Centro at Rua da Quitanda, 49, is open for lunch during weekdays.

Jobi

Avenida Ataulfo de Paiva, 1166; tel: 21-2274 0547; daily L and D. $

Pizzaria Guanabara

Avenida Ataulfo de Paiva, 1228; tel: 21-2294 0797; daily L and D. $$

The Guanabara, with a relaxed family atmosphere, is one of Rio's classic pizzerias. It's open late, often busy until it closes, and is popular with artists and old-school *carioca* bohemians. Pizza can also be ordered by the slice.

Plataforma

Rua Adalberto Ferreira, 32; tel: 21-2274 4022; www.plataforma.com; daily L and D. $$$

This traditional *churrascaria*, opened in 1979, attracts huge numbers of tourists to its giant dining room. Specialties include *galeto* (barbecued chicken) and steaks with traditional side dishes. Within the same premises, there's a bar named in honor of Tom Jobim and at night there are samba and folkloric shows upstairs.

Santa Teresa

Aprazível

Rua Aprazível, 62; tel: 21-2508 9174; www.aprazivel.com.br; Tue–Sat L and D, Sun L. $$$

This gourmet experience has panoramic views of Downtown Rio from a renovated manor house with rustic-chic decor. Tables are dotted around the house and gardens. The focus is on contemporary Brazilian cuisine, where regional dishes are given a modern twist. There's a good choice of artisan beers and a large selection of barrel-aged *cachaças*.

Armazém São Thiago

Rua Áurea 26; tel: 21-2232 0822; www.armazemsaothiago.com.br; daily L and D. $$

Founded in 1919 by a Spanish immigrant, and originally run as a store selling wines, olive oil and salt cod, this bohemian bar (also known as Bar do Gomez) retains its original decoration and feel. Apart from beers and *caipirinhas*, it offers a range of classic Brazilian bar appetizers. It buzzes with the young and arty in the evenings and at weekends so come early if you want a seat inside.

Goya Beira

Largo das Neves, 13; tel: 21-2232 5751; daily D. $

Open only in the evenings, this traditional little bar overlooks a bucolic square, off the beaten track. It's a simple sort of place where the locals hang out and beers come in liter bottles with little glasses. To eat, there are classic appetizers, like *aipim com carne seca* (fried manioc with salted beef).

Urca

Bar Urca

Rua Cândido Gaffré, 205; tel: 21-2295 8744; www.barurca.com.br; daily B, L and D. $$

Right at the end of Urca and overlooking Botafogo Bay, Bar Urca is split into two parts. At street level, you order bottles of beer and Brazilian bar snacks, like *empanadas*, to take onto the seawall, where a young crowd congregates. Upstairs, there's a formal restaurant specializing in seafood.

Flor da Urca

Rua Marechal Cantuária, 148; tel: 21-2541 7674; Mon–Sat B, L and D. $

Large portions of grilled meat, with rice, beans and salad, are served in this very traditional eatery. Decoration is unfussy with tiled walls, specials on the blackboard and a fridge stocked full of beers. You'll also get coffees and *lanches* (snacks) here.

Garota da Urca

Avenida João Luís Alves, 56; tel: 21-2541 8585; daily L and D. $$

Part of a small chain of *botecos*, which also includes Garota de Ipanema (see page 77), this is a casual spot for a beer, typical Brazilian food, including steaks, and pizza. It opens onto the waterfront overlooking the tiny Praia da Urca, with Corcovado Mountain rising up from the sea in the background.

NIGHTLIFE

Rio de Janeiro is proudly nocturnal, with a wide variety of activities, from big, brassy nightclubs and chic discos to friendly jazz bars and informal samba clubs. For the more upscale drinking and dancing venues, head to the hotel bars in Santa Teresa, Copacabana or Ipanema. If you want a real wild night deserving of a city like Rio, then head to Lapa on a weekend and let the kinetic energy and hoards of revelers sweep you away. The best way to find out what's on is to ask someone local on your arrival or visit www.ingresso.com.br/rio-de-janeiro.

Theater

Oi Casa Grande
Avenida Afrânio de Melo Franco, 290; tel: 21-3114 3712; www.oicasagrande.oi.com.br; bus: 128.
This theater, adjacent to Shopping Leblon, has been staging Brazilian and international musical productions and other performances since 1966.

Teatro Municipal
Praça Florianao; tel: 21-2332 919l; www.theatromunicipal.rj.gov.br; metro: ML1, ML2 at Cinelandia.
This grand opera house is one of Rio's prized architectural and cultural monuments. The entrance and exterior are copies of the Paris Opera house, and everyone from Toscanini to Baryshnikov to Pavarotti has graced its stage.

Teatro Poeira
Rua São João Batista, 104; tel: 21-2537 8053; www.teatropoeira.com.br; bus: 511.
Located in Botafogo, the Ministry of Culture sponsors the shows performed here, which embrace the concept of a 'living theater', open to collaboration and experimentation.

Dance

Estudantina Musical
Praça Tiradentes, 79; tel: 21-2232 1149; www.estudantinamusical.com.br; metro ML1, ML2 at Carioca; Tue–Sat 8pm–4am.
This dance hall is a slice of Old Rio that will transport you back to the 1930s. Even if you don't like dancing, this casual place may change your mind. Things really get going around midnight.

Samba Salgueiro
Rua Silva Téles, 104; tel: 21-2238 9226; www.salgueiro.com.br; take taxi; Sat 10pm–4am.
This samba school, located in Tijuca, starts prepping for Carnival months in advance. Every Saturday they open their doors for a peak at rehearsals, and it's a great excuse to go join in the action.

Movies

Cine Estacão Laura Alvim
Avenida Vieira Souto, 176; tel: 21-2267 1647; metro: ML1 at General Osório.
This intimate, three-screen theater, located in a cultural center in Ipanema,

Live music at the Santo Scenarium bar, next to Rio Scenarium

shows its fair share of Hollywood block-busters, but also offers up classics and art films.

Bars and nightclubs

Acadamia de Cachaca

Rua Conde de Bernadotte, 26; tel: 21-2239 1542; www.academiadacachaca.com.br; bus: 464; daily noon–2am, Sun until 1am.

Located in a commercial area in Leblon, this bar serves what many believe to be the best *caipirinhas* in Rio. They only use top-quality *cachaça* (of which the founder supposedly had 2,000 bottles in his personal collection). They have a regular menu of bar food as well as their much-ballyhooed *feijoada*.

Bar Dos Descasados

Rua Alm. Alexandrino, 660; tel: 21-3380 0240; www.santa-teresa-hotel.com; bus: 006, 007, 014; daily 12.30pm–midnight.

Situated in the Hotel Santa Teresa, this is one of the most intimate and impeccably designed bars in Rio. The open-air, dimly lit space is fantastic and there's no better vantage point to watch the sun set over Guanabara Bay. Live jazz some nights.

Bar do Gomes

Rua Áurea, 26; tel: 21-2232 0822; bus: 014; Mon–Thu noon–midnight, Fri–Sat noon–1am, Sun noon–10pm.

This local institution popular has got everything a great neighborhood bar should have: history, character and locally brewed beer, plus tasty, snacks, meat platters and sandwiches.

Blue Agave

Rua Vinícius de Moraes, 68; tel: 21-3592 9271; metro: ML1 at Gen. Osório; bus: 413, 426, 435; daily noon–2am.

Run by three California expats, Blue Agave is a throwback to the great beachside watering holes of Southern California. There's a good selection of tacos on offer, including the king of all meats: *al pastor*. As for the drinks, go straight for the margaritas. There's a second location at Rua Aires de Saldanha, 21, in Copacabana.

Carioca da Gema

Avenida Mem de Sá, 79; tel: 21-2221 0043; metro: ML1, ML2 at Cinelândia; bus: 006, 014, 178; Mon–Fri 7pm–4am, Sat–Sun 9pm–4am.

Located in the heart of Lapa, just a couple blocks from the arches, this is popular with folks who want to dance to live samba. The ambience is perfect, with exposed brick walls and three floors connected by a twisting wooden staircase. It also serves pizza.

Rio Scenarium

Rua do Lavradio, 20; tel: 21-3147 9000; www.rioscenarium.com.br; metro: ML1, ML2 at Carioca; Tue–Fri 7.30pm–4.30am, Sat 8pm–4am.

Housed in an old colonial building on a cobble street, this is one of Rio's must-visit clubs. Spread over three floors, the decor is wall-to-wall kitsch. Live samba and bossa nova bands perform nightly. It's about as family-friendly a club is you are likely to find anywhere in Rio.

Street scene on a rainy day in the Centro

A–Z

A

Addresses

Travelers from the US will find the street numbers to be refreshingly familiar, with odd number addresses on one side and even numbers on the other. Unlike many other South American metropolises, there is no elaborate grid system or otherwise confounding street address system. The main neighborhoods are easily accessible via bus or metro.

The following will help you understand Brazilian addresses and place names:

Al. or **Alameda** = lane
Andar = floor, story
Av. or **Avenida** = avenue
Casa = house
Centro = the central downtown business district, also frequently referred to as a *cidade* (the city)
Cj or **Conjunto** = a suite of rooms, or sometimes a group of buildings
Estr or **Estrada** = road or highway
Fazenda = ranch, also a lodge
Lgo or Largo = square or plaza
Lote = lot
Pça or **Praça** = square or plaza
Praia = beach
Rio = river
Rod or **Rodovia** = highway
R or **Rua** = street
Sala = room

Age restrictions

Like in most Latin-American countries, the official drinking age is 18.

B

Budgeting for your trip

The unit of currency in Brazil is the real (R$; plural, reais).

Most Latin American economies tend to be volatile, so what is true today may not necessarily be so when you get to Brazil. For example, Rio was a cheap getaway during much of the 1980s, but became one of the world's most expensive cities in the early 1990s. Since currency reform in 1994, prices have tended to be relatively stable. However, 2015 saw a sharp depreciation in Brazil's currency, and a recession ensued. The weak economy means Brazil once again offers excellent value to North American and European visitors. But bear in mind locals aren't pleased with this turn of events, and stress levels regarding Brazil's economic future are high. Best not to rub it in.

Here is a general price table, in US dollars, to help you plan your trip:
A beer **US$1–3**
A glass of house wine **US$2–5**
Main course at a budget, moderate and expensive restaurant **US$4–6**, **US$8–15**, **US$20–30**

Playing cards on the street in Lapa

Room in a cheap, moderate and deluxe hotel **US$40–50**, **US$75–150**, **US$150** and over

Taxi from airport to main destination **US$15–20**

Single bus ticket **US$1**

Single Metro ticket **US$1**

Accommodation. In general, hotels are reasonably priced. Most, but not all, include breakfast in the price of the room. And with the devaluation of the real, there is no better time than now to book a room in a high-end hotel. Even the Copacabana Palace, one of the most luxurious hotels in the world, has weekday rates that rival mid-range accommodations in the US.

Eating out. The cost of dining in Rio, when compared to major cities in Europe and the US, is very reasonable. Many restaurants have attractively priced *pratos do dia* menus at lunchtime, and some *churrascarias* (barbecue restaurants) offer daytime discounts. The *por kilo* buffet-style restaurants are always a good bet for travelers on a budget. And for those with cash to burn, it's possible to get a seat at the chef's table in a Michelin-starred restaurant for around US$150.

Transportation. Flights to Brazil are fairly expensive, especially in high season. Transportation on the ground is quite reasonable; local and intra-state buses are very cheap, and taxis are an affordable option for getting around the city. Remember when traveling within Brazil that the country is larger than the USA. The choice can often be 48 hours on a bus or three hours on a plane. If you are going to be traveling in Brazil, look at getting an air-pass (www.brol.com/airpass) prior to your arrival. Brazil also has some low-cost airlines such as Gol (www.voegol.com.br) and Azul (www.azul.com.br).

Children

Cariocas are very family-oriented, and the city offers much beach fun for the whole family. The zoo and outdoor markets are also great for kids. Most attractions offer a discount for children, often around 50 percent off. Parents who want to take a breather will find that the more upscale hotels, such as the Copacabana Palace, offer babysitting services.

Clothing

Rio is a beach city, and *cariocas* are beach people. For these reasons board shorts, flip-flops and even string bikinis are allowed almost anywhere during the day. However, going out at night might require more than a T-shirt and shorts, depending on the venue. Travelers enjoying a meal in a fancy hotel or upscale neighborhood like Leblon should follow the rules of decorum and dress accordingly – but even these places are pretty relaxed. A certain degree of modesty is expected when visiting historic churches, however.

If you visit Rio during its summer, you may need an umbrella, or at least a cap or hat. Locals rarely wear raincoats because they're too hot. For Rio's winter, pack a light jumper.

Crowds at Ipanema beach

Crime and safety

The horror stories that have been published in the past that make Rio sound like a tropical Wild West are a bit exaggerated. Petty crime, as in all the world's major cities where tourists congregate, remains a problem, and it's best to take the necessary precautions. Store your valuables in the hotel safe. Take nothing of value to the beach, where sneaky thieves take advantage of careless or unwary tourists. An old trick is for a kid to approach you from one side and ask you the time; he'll pretend not to understand, while behind you one of his partners is picking you clean. More subtly, someone might ask you to guard his shirt while he goes swimming; he tosses the shirt casually over your belongings, and on his return scoops up the lot. You should also beware of pickpockets in crowds and keep wallets and bags in front of you. Stay clear of lonely beaches and unlit streets, and avoid displays of jewelry.

Note that possession of even small quantities of drugs can bring up to two years' imprisonment; the authorities make little distinction between marijuana, pills or hard drugs.

Keep safe in the water by remembering that appearances are often deceptive – an apparently mild beach may have a strong undertow. So if the lifeguard hoists a red flag, stay out of the water, no matter how inviting it looks. Never allow children to swim unattended.

Customs regulations

International passengers may purchase duty-free goods for a total of US$500 or the equivalent in another currency on arrival in Brazil, including a restricted amount of alcoholic beverages.

A non-resident may import an unlimited amount of foreign currency and travelers' checks and a reasonable amount of Brazilian reais, but must declare any amount above R$10,000.

Disabled travelers

This is a touchy subject, especially for locals with disabilities. While it's true that most of Rio's modern hotels and restaurants accommodate wheelchairs, the city streets are another matter. It's certainly possible to navigate the beaches of the Zona Sul in a wheelchair, but there is almost no direct access. Plus, the poor nature of streets in Rio (cracked sidewalks and potholes galore) means that getting around can be an uphill battle. Also, certain neighborhoods situated on hillsides, such as Santa Teresa, may prove difficult for wheelchair-users to navigate, and accommodation options (like B&Bs run out of homes) may lack ramps.

However, public transport systems, such as the metro and bus, have been modernized to accommodate passengers with disabilities. Both Christ the Redeemer and the Sugarloaf have disabled access. Taxi company Especial Coop

Military police at the Curvelo station in Santa Teresa

Taxi (www.especialcooptaxirj.com.br) specializes in transportation for passengers with limited mobility. Organizations in Brazil lobbying for better conditions include the IBDD (Brazilian Institute for the Rights of the Disabled Person; www.idealist.org).

E

Electricity

In most places in Rio the current is 110-volts, 60 cycles (the same as in the US). However, some hotels have 220-volt outlets; they are usually marked.

Embassies and consulates

Many consulates and commercial missions operate in the former capital. All embassies are now based in Brasília.

Australia (Honorary Consul): Avenida Presidente Wilson, 231/23, Centro; tel: 21-3824 4624; email: honconau@terra.com.br.

Canada: Avenida Atlântica, 1130, 5th floor, Atlântica Business Center, Copacabana; tel: 21-2543 3004; email: rio@international.gc.ca.

UK (also Ireland and New Zealand): Praia do Flamengo, 284, 2nd floor, Flamengo; tel: 21-2555 9600; email: bcg.rj@fco.gov.uk.

US Avenida Presidente Wilson, 147; tel: 21-3823 2000; www.riodejaneiro.usconsulate.gov.

Emergencies

The phone numbers for use in an emergency (*emergência*) are:

Police: **190**
Ambulance: **192**
Fire: **193**

The police on the street, although they have the duties of municipal police, are members of the military police force (*Polícia Militar*; PM). The police are generally patient and courteous with foreigners. If you have a problem, go to one of the many blue-and-white octagonal police posts (marked PM–RIO). The Rio Tourist Police office is in front of the Teatro Casa Grande on Avenida Afrânio de Melo Franco, s/n in Leblon (tel: 21-3399 7170).

Etiquette

Brazil is relaxed when it comes to dress. Still, those who are invited into someone's home for dinner or a get-together will want to be on the safe side and dress the same way they would for a similar meeting at home (but even then they'll likely find themselves overdressed for the occasion).

It's customary when making introductions for men and women to shake hands and exchange a kiss on the cheek. With men, shaking hands (and possibly a pat on the back) is appropriate.

There's no need to get hung up on etiquette in Rio. As mentioned earlier, *cariocas* are mostly informal beach people that tend to welcome visitors with open arms. That said, always remember that the 'A-OK' sign that's so common in the United States is actually an insulting gesture in Rio.

Enjoying a chope at Carnival

F

Festivals and events

1 January New Year's Day and Festa da Iemanjá (Reveillon): Rio's homage to Iemanjá, the goddess of the sea; takes place on and around Copacabana beach.

20 January Dia de São Sebastião: A celebration of St Sebastian, Rio's patron saint.

February/March Carnival: movable feast that starts on the Friday before Shrove Tuesday and comes to a close on Ash Wednesday.

1 March Dia da Fundação da Cidade: Celebration of the city's founding in 1565 by Estácio de Sá.

March/April Sexta-feira da Paixão: Good Friday.

21 April Tiradentes: National holiday.

1 May Labour Day National holiday.

June Festas Juninas (June Festivals): Celebration of saints Anthony, Peter and John. Rio marathon.

3 July Festa do São Pedro do Mar: Festival honoring St Peter, the patron saint of fishermen.

August Grande Premio do Brasil: Brazil's most important horserace, held at the Hipódromo do Jockey Club Brasileiro.

15 August Festa de Nossa Senhora da Glória do Outeiro: Feast of the Assumption in Glória.

September–October Rio Film Festival.

7 September Dia de Independência do Brasil: Independence Day.

October Festa da Penha: Lively religious festival at Igreja Nossa Senhora da Penha. Brazilian Formula One Grand Prix (São Paulo).

12 October Nossa Senhora Aparaceida: National holiday celebrating the patron saint of Brazil.

2 November All Souls' Day.

15 November Republic Day: National holiday celebrating the proclamation of the Republic.

15 December Summer holidays start.

31 December Celebração de Fim do Ano and Festa de Iemanjá: New Year's Eve and Reveillon.

G

Gay and lesbian travelers

Rio has long proudly declared itself the gay capital of Latin America. Carnival is famous for its gay balls and transvestite parades. Many of Brazil's most popular and important singers, like Daniela Mercury and Gilberto Gil, are openly gay or bisexual, and their adoring public gives the matter little attention. Still, gay people face obstacles in the city, and visitors should not think it the place to lose all sense of proportion and discretion.

Despite an aggressive treatment campaign during the early years of the AIDS epidemic, HIV continues to ravage Brazilians, and *cariocas* in particular. Infection rates have been slowly rising since 2005, and now the country trails only Africa and some parts of Asia in new cases. Safe sex should be a commandment. There are condom giveaways in many nightspots, such as Lapa.

Costumes at Carnival

The gay scene for tourists centers on the Zona Sul (although Lapa also has a very active gay life). The stretch of beach in front of the Copacabana Palace hotel is particularly popular with gay visitors; look for the Rainbow kiosk. (This section of beach is referred to as a Bolsa, 'stock market' – ostensibly because it's popular with locals who are looking for rich husbands!) The gay beach in Ipanema is at the end of Rua Farme do Amoedo. Inland, Botafogo has a strong gay presence, especially along rua Visconde de Silva, where you'll find a number of gay restaurants, bars and nightclubs.

The clubs and discos with large gay followings change from season to season; Some favorites include Le Boy and La Girl (Rua Paul Pompeia, 102), The Week (Rua Sacadura Cabral, 135), La Cueva (Rua Miguel Lemos, 51), and Galeria Café (Rua Teixeira de Melo, 31). The Gay Ball during Carnival (Grande Gala G), held at La Scala in Leblon (Avenida Afrânio de Melo Franco, 296), is legendary.

Health and medical care

Rio, like all of Brazil, is not a great place to get sick, although the private hospitals are excellent. While there is a risk of malaria in certain parts of Brazil, a vacation in Rio holds no special health hazards. You are wise to avoid the tap water, however, and take care that an overdose of sun on the first few days doesn't spoil the rest of your stay.

Most hotels can help put you in contact with doctors who speak English (or French, German or Spanish); you can also ask your consulate for a list of doctors and clinics. Municipal hospitals with round-the-clock emergency rooms include:

Miguel Couto, Rua Mario Ribeiro, 117 (Lagoa); tel: 21-3111 3746.

Rocha Maia, Rua General Severiano, 91 (Botafogo); tel: 21-2295 2295.

Souza Aguiar, Praça da República, 111 (Centro); tel: 21-3111 2622.

Pharmacies and drug stores can be found throughout the city. *Drogarias* sell, among other things, many familiar patent medicines (*remédios*), but only *farmácias* are allowed to fill prescriptions and give injections. Droga Raia is one of the largest pharmacy chains in the city and has locations at: Avenida Ataulfo de Paiva, 1282 (Leblon); Rua Visconde de Pirajá, 210 (Ipanema), Avenida N.S. Senhora de Copacaba, 787 (Copacabana), and Rua Marquês de Abrantes, 143. These locations are open until at least 11pm. They also have a 24-hour store in Barro de Tijuca at Avenida Dos Americas, 7000. Drogaria Peixoto is another option that has a 24-hour location at Rua Figueiredo de Magalhães, 615 (Copacabana).

No vaccinations are required for Rio unless you are arriving from, or have recently visited, countries infected with certain serious diseases (including cholera and yellow fever); again the latest regulations can be found at your local Brazilian consulate.

Service at the NS do Rosario church

Hours and holidays

Government offices are usually open weekdays 8am–5pm, but some open as late as 11am. Shops and stores are generally open from 9am–6pm, but in certain neighborhoods they have longer hours, sometimes opening before 8am and closing around 10pm. Some businesses close for lunch between noon and 2pm. Museums tend to close on Monday. Their weekday hours are 10am or noon to 5 or 6pm; weekends they open 2 or 3pm to 5 or 6pm. Public holidays are as follows:

1 January New Year's Day
20 January St Sebastian's Feast Day (*São Sebastião*)
February/March Carnival
March/April Good Friday/Easter
21 April Tiradentes
1 May Labor Day
June Corpus Christi
7 September Independence Day (*Dia de Independência do Brasil*)
12 October Our Lady of the Apparition
2 November All Souls' Day
15 November Proclamation of Brazilian Republic
25 December Christmas

Internet facilities

The age of the internet café is slowly coming to a close (at least in Rio), in large part due to the ubiquity of Wi-Fi as well as the fact that all modern mobile devices have internet capability. Still, internet facilities do exist in the city, and most charge around R$5 per hour. Some good options include Cyber Copa Café in Copacabana (Avenida Nossa Sra. De Copacabana, 1077), Central Fone in Centro (Avenida Trez de Maio, 33) and Cyber Gol in Catete (Rua do Catete, 122).

M

Media

Major newspapers, including the *International Herald Tribune*, *Miami Herald*, *USA Today* and the international editions of *Time* and *Newsweek* are available in hotels and at newsstands. Entertainment listings are found in the Portuguese-language dailies, notably *O Globo* (www.oglobo.globo.com) and *Jornal do Brasil* (www.jb.com.br), and the weekly news magazine, *Vejá* (www.veja.abril.com.br) Most hotels have cable, which has CNN, Bloomberg TV and BBC World, as well as other international satellite services.

Money

Currency

In an attempt to halt inflation in Brazil, the government pegged the Brazilian currency, the real (R$, plural reais), to the US dollar on its launch in 1994. In 1999 the real was allowed to trade freely against other international currencies. Banknotes: R$1, R$5, R$10, R$50 and R$100; coins: 1, 5, 10, 25 and 50 centavos.

Casas de câmbio are small currency exchange offices and often travel agencies. Your hotel can change money, but

Christ the Redeemer

at a rate that will probably be worse than the one you can get at *casas de câmbio* or banks. Currency can be changed at banks Mon–Fri 10am–4.30pm; *casas de câmbio* are generally open Mon–Sat 8am–6pm. Major hotels and some restaurants change money on Sunday and holidays, but the rate suffers. The best rate is often found at the ATM machines, many of which operate 24 hours. Considering the instability of the Brazilian economy, travelers should expect to see fluctuations in exchange rates.

Credit cards

Most major hotels, restaurants, shops and car-hire agencies accept the major credit cards, but there is still some uncertainty as to which cards they take. For example, some will take Visa but not MasterCard and vice versa, so if it matters, check first. That said, card payments are becoming more and more common, and now many smaller restaurants, stores and markets accept credit and debit cards.

ATMs

ATM machines (*caixas automáticas*) are widespread and often the safest and best way to get local currency. Not all machines, especially inside banks where there may be many different machines, are linked to the international network, but those that are, are clearly marked, so don't panic if the first machine you try only takes Brazilian cards. HSBC ATMs work with most cards, and these machines give out the maximum amount of R$1,000.

Tipping

A 10 percent service charge is generally included in restaurant bills. If not, that amount should be left for acceptable service. For bellboys on errands, the odd coin is appropriate. Taxi drivers do not receive tips so round up the fare. Some further guidelines, in dollar equivalents:

Hotel porter, per bag **US$1**
Maid, per week **US$10**
Tour guide **US$3–5**

Post

Post offices (*correios*) are found all over town: look for the yellow sign ECT (Empresa Brasileira de Correios e Telégrafos; www.correios.com.br). The post office at Rio de Janeiro international airport is open 24 hours a day. Branch offices tend to stay open from 8am to 6pm or 8pm, Monday to Friday, and 8am–noon on Saturday. If you're still a letter-writing romantic, you'll spend about R$2 to send a postcard or letter (up to 10g) internationally. Service has improved in recent years, and Brazil's post office now offers internet and electronic-posting services.

Religion

Brazil has the largest Roman Catholic population in the world, but many other religions are active as well. The number of adherents to evangelical Protestant denominations has increased dramati-

Rocinha favela

cally in recent years, and a number of African religions continue to thrive as well. Religious services are regularly held in several languages, including English, French, German, Swedish, Arabic and Chinese.

The monthly booklets issued by the municipal tourism organisation, Riotur, list the times and places for Catholic, Protestant and Jewish services, as well as for the two leading Afro-Brazilian religions, Umbanda and Candomblé.

Smoking

Rio has followed the lead of most other major international cities in that smoking is generally prohibited indoors in public places. However, you'll see plenty of folks puffing away on the city streets as well as the beaches, and many hotels still offers smoking rooms. So smokers needn't be scared off completely.

Telephones

Brazil's country code is 55, and the Rio city code is 21. The international service works well. Public telephones are mounted in protective domes commonly called *orelhões* ('big ears'). The orange ones are for local calls, the blue (marked DDD) for long-distance. Phone cards are sold at most newsstands and many pharmacies and grocery stores. The number for the operator is 100.

You can dial direct (DDI), which is cheaper, to most countries in the world, by first dialing 00, followed by the long distance operator code (21 for Embratel or 23 for Intelig) and then the country's own code, followed by the area code and the number you want to contact. Should the area code start with a zero, the zero must be dropped. Therefore the number of the Brazilian Embassy in central London, for example, is 00-(21 or 23)-44-20 7747 4500.

When calling from Rio to the rest of Brazil you must also include the code of a long-distance operator, which can be confusing as the Embratel code, 21, is the same as that of the city of Rio.

For operator-assisted long-distance calls, phone 101; for overseas calls, phone 000-111 or 000-333. Hotels in Rio may allow their guests to make local calls free, but they add a stiff service charge to the tariff for international calls. At the airports and several other key locations, there are public telephone offices from which you can make long-distance and overseas calls. Internet Fone Rio, a call center, is located in Copacabana at Rua Miguel Lemos and is open until 11pm on weekends.

It is possible to use foreign cellular phones and smartphones within Brazil, but you should first check with your service provider as to exactly what types of roaming charges you'll likely incur. To dial internationally from a cell, you may have to follow the same procedure as for a landline and choose a long distance oper-

Training at a public outdoor gym on Arpoador beach

ator. For example 00 (for international) followed by 21 (for Embratel), followed by the number of the country you wish to talk to and the full telephone number.

If you plan to make lots of local calls in Brazil it may be worth getting a Brazilian SIM card for your phone. All main mobile operators in Brazil offer a SIM card-only package and most have stores in the major shopping centers where you can have your phone connected. Renting a handset is another option.

Country codes: Australia 61; Canada 1; Ireland 353; New Zealand 64; South Africa 27; UK 44; US 1.

Time zones

Rio Standard Time is 3 hours behind Greenwich Mean Time. During Brazilian summer (Nov–Feb), the clock is advanced 1 hour in Rio.

Toilets

Public conveniences are rare in Rio, but you can always find facilities in hotels, restaurants and bars. There's no problem walking in to a bar or restaurant just to use the facilities. If there's an attendant on duty, a tip is expected. Ladies is *Senhoras* or *Damas*; Gentlemen is *Homens* or, sometimes, *Cavalheiros*. Signs are often abbreviated to 'S' and 'H' ('She' and 'He', if you forget). Also, remember that due to Brazil's plumbing system, toilet paper should always be tossed in the wastebasket rather than flushed.

Tourist information

For tourist information once you have arrived in Brazil, contact one of the following:

Riotur (city tourism authority): Praça Pio X 119, 9º, Centro; tel: 21-2976 7301; www.rio.rj.gov.br/riotur. Information can be obtained at the Riotur booths at the international airport (daily 6am–10pm), and in Copacabana at Avenida Princesa Isabel, 183; tel: 21-2271 7000 (Mon–Fri 9am–6pm).

SETUR-RJ & TurisRio (government office covering the State of Rio de Janeiro): Rua Uruguaiana, 118, Centro; tel: 21-3803 9350; www.rio.com.br/web/setur.

Tours and guides

The tour operators who specialize in the region tend to be very knowledgeable and can help put together the best programs and most complex itineraries, whether you are just visiting Rio or touring the whole of Brazil. It does not even matter if you haven't purchased your air ticket from them.

In the UK, folks can find tour operators to Brazil via the Latin American Travel Association (www.lata.org) and the Visit Brazil Travel Association (www.vibrata.org). A list of UK operators can also be found on the Brazilian Embassy website (www.brazil.org.uk) and most reputable US operators can be found via the American Society of Travel Agents (www.asta.org).

A few specific tour companies within Rio include Rio Adventures (tel: 21-2705 5747; www.rioadventures.com), which specializes in adventure sports such as skydiving and paragliding; Rio by Bike (tel: 968 718 933; www.riobybike.com), specializing in bicycle tours; and Eat Rio (www.eatrio.net), a company offering gastronomic tours of the city.

Transportation

Getting there
By air

Because of demand, most flights, especially from Europe, go via São Paulo. US gateway cities for travel to Rio include Los Angeles, Miami, Houston, Washington and New York. American Airlines and TAM fly directly to Rio from New York and Miami. From Canada, the gateway city is Toronto, with Air Canada.

From the UK, direct flights with British Airways depart from London. Most other major European capitals and airlines also serve Rio and the highest number of flights is between Portugal and Brazil with TAP, who offer direct flights from Lisbon to Rio and São Paulo, as well as Brasiliá, Belo Horizonte, Salvador, Recife, Natal and Fortaleza.

From Australia and New Zealand, flights originate in Sydney and often stop in Auckland, with connections via Buenos Aires, Santiago or Los Angeles. Flights from Johannesburg, South Africa, stop in São Paulo.

Brazil's main international carriers is TAM (www.tam.com.br).

On arrival

Rio's international airport is RIOgaleão–Antonio Carlos Jobim International Airport (known simply as 'Galeão'), on Ilha do Governado (tel: 21-3004 6050). The airport has two terminals that are linked by a moving walkway. Terminal 2, is home to Tam, Lufthansa and many of the Star Alliance partners such as United and Avianca. Most other international airlines use Terminal 1. Just beyond the customs hall, and this is true for both terminals, are basic information desks as well as desks operated by Riotur, Rio's official tourist agency, where multilingual receptionists answer questions, distribute pamphlets, and help with hotel reservations. The desks are 24 hours, except the two in the arrivals terminal, which close at 10pm and opens at 6am. There's an airport call center (tel: 21-3004 6050), which offers flight information. The airport has banks for changing money and a selection of ATM machines. On leaving Brazil there is no bank beyond passport control (flight side) to change reais back into other currencies. The duty-free stores now finally accept reais but it's still best to spend or get rid of your reais at the shops before going through passport control.

Immediately outside the customs hall are the desks of the authorized taxi companies that charge standard fares from the airport according to destination; you pay on the spot in advance and give the receipt to the driver. You can also prepay for your return taxi ride to the airport, something worth considering given the

Copacabana Metro station

generous discounts offered. The trip to the business center takes 30 to 40 minutes, to the beach zone, up to an hour if you arrive during the morning rush hour. Taxis are not expensive and are the best and safest way to get to your accommodation.

A cheaper way to reach central Rio and the beach hotels is by bus. A convenient blue bus, called a *frescão*, travels from the international airport to Santos Dumont airport and then along the beaches. They all have air-conditioning and Wi-Fi and are good value for the service. The returning bus passes along the beaches, but stops are not well indicated, and the bus passes infrequently. There is also a shuttle van service between the airport and many of the main hotels (tel: 21-7842 2490; www.shuttlerio.com.br). An airport tax is levied on departure – this may or may not have been included in your ticket. Payment can be made either in dollars or reais.

Santos Dumont Airport, Rio's second airport, is close to the center. Most flights are between Rio and São Paulo with other domestic services operating from the international airport. To get there from the Zona Sul resorts, take any air-conditioned bus going to the center of Rio – they'll let you off within easy walking distance of the airport.

Getting around
By bus
Thousands of city buses race through the streets of Rio when traffic permits; if the traffic is jammed, they race their engines in protest. By some estimates, there are over 800 routes, which might explain why no bus maps of Rio are available. However, in preparation for the 2016 games, the city put together a transport map on its official website (www.rio2016.com). While the interactive map is useful, the bus information provided is not nearly as detailed as it could be. It's always best to ask advice on which bus to catch, and where. Avoid rush hours (8–10am and 5–7pm), travel by bus after dark only when necessary, and beware of pickpockets at all times. Also, hold on for dear life.

You normally enter a city bus through the rear door and leave at the front. A conductor sits near the rear door by a turnstile. For luxury public transport, ride the *frescões* (literally, 'big cool ones'), the air-conditioned buses linking the beach areas with central Rio. The destination is posted in the right-hand front window. On the journey into town, these buses go to the central Menezes Cortês bus station near Praça XV. On the return trip, the destinations cover most of the beach communities from Leme to São Conrado and even beyond. The *frescões* pull over at any bus stop on a signal from a passenger or potential passenger.

Buses are also linked to the various Metro stations and can be included in the fare. Details and a map of the bus services linked to the Metro can be found at www.metrorio.com.br.

Metro
Rio's subway (www.metrorio.com.br) system didn't go into operation until 1979.

Santa Teresa tram mural

Early in 1982, Line One was completed, and now it runs from Tijuca at Terminal Urguai to Praça General Osório in Ipanema. Special buses link the station at General Osório with Leblon, Gávea and Barra. Line Two runs from Botafogo past centro and up to Pavuna, in the Zona Norte. Rio's clean, safe, efficient subway runs from 5am–midnight Monday to Saturday, and on Sunday from 7am–11pm. It runs 24 hours during Carnival.

Payment is by MetrôRio cards, and a single ride costs R$3.70. Prepaid cards are available at a minimum charge of R$5. The metro is by far the quickest and most comfortable way to get from Copacabana to the city center.

By tram

Only one tram line still functions in Rio, and it's well worth the trouble, even if only for the nostalgia factor. The terminal is near Largo da Carioca, and the ancient trams cross the arches high above the Lapa section on the way up to suburban Santa Teresa. Unfortunately, due to an accident in 2011, the tram has been mostly suspended; it currently only runs between two points: centro and Largo do Curvelo in Santa Teresa. However, it is set to reopen in full by the 2016 Olympics.

Taxis

Rio's yellow taxis are ubiquitous. There are taxi stands at the airports and at the ferry and railway stations. Except in a rainstorm, the supply of taxis exceeds the demand and they can be hailed at any point. Taxis in Rio are cheap and a much better option for visitors than the buses.

As well as the yellow taxis, Rio also has an excellent radio taxi service. The main companies, which can also provide the simplest way to get to the airport, are Aerocoop (tel: 21-3078 5050; www.aerocoop.com.br), Cooparioca (tel: 2158-1818; www.cooparioca.com.br), Coopsind (tel: 21-2189 4503; www.riocoopsind.com.br) and the mobile app Easy Taxi (www.easytaxi.com), which services Rio De Janeiro. Especial Coop Taxi (tel: 21-3295 9606; www.especialcooptaxirj.com.br) has specially equipped vehicles to accommodate passengers with disabilities.

By ferry

Every day more than 150,000 passengers ride the ferries, run by CCR Barcas (www.barcas-sa.com.br) between Rio de Janeiro and Niterói, a 20-minute voyage that costs around R$5. Most of the passengers are commuters who ignore the sea breezes and inspiring views.

Driving

The obvious question is: why drive? Local drivers are not noted for their courtesy, nor are they terribly interested in obeying signals and laws. Even bus drivers sometimes run red lights, especially late at night. Cars may pass you on either side. Pedestrians need to be extremely cautious: they have the lowest priority of all moving objects in Rio.

Renting a car in Rio can be expensive. If you're staying in the city, there's no reason to hire a car; do so only for excursions. International and local car-hire agencies have offices at the airports,

The Niterói ferry

in the business center, and in Copacabana, Ipanema, Leblon and other tourist areas. Drivers must be 18 and have held a valid licence for at least two years; you'll also need a credit card and, often, your passport. Third-party insurance is required and usually included in the charge, but make sure the price you are quoted reflects this condition. Collision insurance is a sizable extra. The fine print on contracts always hides clauses that can be troublesome in case of an accident. Read the contract carefully.

You can hire a car from a major company (Localiza, Unidas) at the international airport or in the Zona Sul; likewise Hertz, Avis and Budget are based in Copacabana as well as at the airport. Charges start from US$20 a day for a basic package.

The speed limit is 80kph (50mph) on all highways, including expressways, 60kph (37mph) in towns.

Gas is more expensive than in the US and comparable to or lower than prices in Europe. Service stations are usually open at night and on Sunday. Make sure that the attendant sets the fuel meter back to zero before filling your tank, and that he uses the correct fuel. Many cars in Brazil run on alcohol-based fuel.

Finding a space is very difficult, especially in the beach areas. Illegal triple parking in the street is quite common. Rio has no parking meters, but some areas have parking wardens (*guardadores autônomos*) who collect a posted fee for two hours' parking. Elsewhere, neighborhood children or old men often supervise parking, expecting a fee for watching over the car. Hotel parking, in guarded areas, can be comparatively expensive.

Visas and passports

Citizens of Australia, Canada, New Zealand and the US require a visa to enter Brazil; even if your airline lets you board, you'll be sent back if you don't have one. Citizens of these countries should plan on obtaining their visas at least one month before arrival in Brazil. Citizens of the UK and most European countries at the time of writing need only a valid passport to enter Brazil, but this may change. Check with your local Brazilian consulate.

Weights and measures

Brazil uses the metric system.

Women travelers

In general, Rio is a safe destination for women traveling alone. Having said that, it is important to stay clear of downtown at night (except for Lapa on weekends), avoid buses at night, and stick to well-lit areas with plenty of people around. Petty criminals seem to target visitors regardless of gender, so conspicuous tourists will probably stand out as ripe for a wallet, purse or smartphone snatch. Remember to always be alert and aware of your surroundings.

Lucky ribbons

LANGUAGE

Although Portuguese, not Spanish, is the language of Brazil, a knowledge of Spanish will go a long way. You will recognize many similar words, and some Brazilians will understand you if you speak in Spanish. You will, however, find it difficult to understand them. Although many upper-class Brazilians know at least some English or French and are eager to practice on foreign visitors, don't expect people on the street to speak your language. An effort by a foreigner to learn the local language is always appreciated. Pronunciation can be confusing. For example, 'r' is pronounced 'h,' so that 'Rio' sounds like 'Hee-o.'

Addressing people

First names are used a great deal in Brazil. In many situations in which English-speakers would use a title and surname, Brazilians often use a first name with the title of respect: *Senhor* for men (written *Sr* and usually shortened to *Seu* in spoken Portuguese) and *Senhora* (written *Sra*) or *Dona* (used only with first name) for women.

There are three second-person pronoun forms in Portuguese. Stick to *você*, equivalent to 'you,' and you will be all right. *O senhor* (for men) or *a senhora* (for women) is used to show respect for someone of a dif- ferent age group or social class, or to be polite to a stranger. As a foreigner, you won't offend anyone if you use the wrong form of address. But if you want to learn when to use the more formal or informal style, observe how others address you, and be guided by that. In some parts of Brazil, mainly the northeast and the south, tu is used a great deal. Originally, in Portugal, *tu* was used among intimate friends and close relatives, but in Brazil, it is equivalent to *você*.

Greetings

Good morning (good afternoon) *Bom dia (boa tarde)*
Good evening (good night) *Boa noite*
How are you? *Como vai você?*
Well, thank you *Bem, obrigado*
Goodbye (very informal and most used) *Tchau*
Goodbye (literally 'until soon') *Até logo*
Goodbye (similar to 'farewell') *Adeus*
My name is (I am) *Meu nome é (Eu sou)*
What is your name? *Como é seu nome?*
Health! (the most common toast) *Saúde*
Do you speak English? *Você fala inglês?*
I don't understand (I didn't under- stand) *Não entendo (Não entendi)*
Do you understand? *Você entende?*

Garota Carioca beachwear

Please repeat more slowly *Por favor repete, mais devagar*
What do you call this (that)? *Como se chama isto (aquilo)?*
How do you say...? *Como se diz...?*
Please *Por favor*
Thank you (very much) *(Muito) Obrigado (or obrigada, if a woman is speaking)*
You're welcome (literally 'it's nothing') *De nada*
Excuse me (to apologize) *Desculpe*
Excuse me (taking leave or to get past someone) *Com licença*

Emergencies

I need... *Eu preciso de...*
a doctor *um medico*
a mechanic *um mecânico*
transportation *condução*
help *ajuda*

Getting around

Where is the...? *Onde é...?*
beach *a praia*
bathroom *o banheiro*
bus station *a rodoviária*
airport *o aeroporto*
train station *a estação de trem*
post office *o correio*
police station *a delegacia de polícia*
ticket office *a bilheteria*
marketplace *o mercado*
street market *feira*
embassy (consulate) *a embaixada (o consulado)*
Where is there a...? *Onde é que tem...?*
currency exchange *uma casa de câmbio*

bank *um banco*
pharmacy *uma farmácia*
bus stop *um ponto de ônibus*
taxi stand *um ponto de taxi*
subway station *uma estação de metrô*
supermarket *um supermercado*
department store *uma loja de departamentos*
boutique *uma boutique*
jeweler *um joalheiro*
hospital *um hospital*
doctor *um médico*
A ticket to... *Uma passagem para...*
I want to go to... *Quero ir para...*
How can I get to...? *Como posso ir para...?*
Please take me to... *Por favor, me leve para...*
Please call a taxi for me *Por favor, chame um taxi para mim*
How long will it take to get there? *Levo quanto tempo para chegar lá?*
Please stop here (Stop!) *Por favor, pare aqui (Pare!)*

Shopping

Do you have...? *Você tem...?*
I want to buy... *Eu quero comprar...*
Can you help me please? *Pode ajudar-me, por favor?*
Where can I buy...? *Onde posso comprar...?*
this (that) *isto (aqui)*
How much does it cost? *Quanto custa? Quanto é?*
a lot, very (many) *muito (muitos)*
a little (few) *um pouco (poucos)*

handbag (purse) *bolsa/saco*
money purse *porta-moedas*
wallet *carteira*

At the hotel

I have a reservation *Tenho uma reserva*
I want to make a reservation *Quero fazer uma reserva*
A single room (A double room) *Um quarto de solteiro (Um quarto de casal)*
With air conditioning *com ar condicionado*
I want to see the room *Quero ver o quarto*
suitcase *mala/bolsa*
room service *serviço de quarto*
key *chave*
the manager *o gerente*

At the restaurant

waiter *garçon*
maître d' *daitre*
The menu (the wine list) *O cardápio (a carta de vinhos)*
breakfast *café da manhã*
lunch *almoço*
supper *jantar*
the house specialty *a especialidade da casa*
carbonated mineral water *água mineral com gás*
uncarbonated mineral water *água mineral sem gás*
coffee *café*
tea *chá*
beer (bottled) *cerveja*

beer (draft) *chope*
white wine (red wine) *vinho branco (vinho tinto)*
a soft drink (juice) *um refrigerante (suco)*
an alcoholic drink *um drink*
a glass of wine *uma taça de vinho*
ice *gelo*
salt *sal*
pepper *pimenta*
sugar *açúcar*
bread *pão*
egg *ovo*
fish *peixe*
crab *caranguejo/aratu*
herring *arenque*
lobster *lavagante*
seafood *marisco*
meat *carne*
beef *carne de boi*
chicken *frango*
ham *presunto*
lamb *borrego*
liver *fígado*
mutton *carneiro*
pork *porco*
stew *guisado*
vegetables *legumes*
potatoes *batatas*
eggplant *beringela*
avocado *abacate*
beans *feijãos*
broad beans *favas*
carrots *cenouras*
garlic *alho*
ginger *gengibre*
lettuce *alface*

Conversation at a restaurant in Lapa

well done *bem passado*
medium rare *ao ponto*
rare *mal passado*
baked *cocido no forno*
homemade *caseiro*
I'm a vegetarian *Eu sou vegetariano/a*
I don't eat meat/fish *Eu não como carne/peixe*
The bill, please *A conta, por favor*
Is service charge included? *Está incluído o serviço?*

Money

bank *banco*
cash *dinheiro*
Do you accept credit cards? *Aceita cartão de crédito?*
Can you cash a traveler's check? *Pode trocar um traveler's check? (cheque de viagem)*
I want to exchange money *Quero trocar dinheiro*
What is the exchange rate? *Qual é o câmbio?*

Time

When? *Quando?*
What time is it? *Que horas são?*
yesterday *ontem*
today *hoje*
tomorrow *amanhã*
this week *esta semana*
last week *a semana passada/*
next week *a semana que vem*
the weekend *o fim de semana*
Monday *segunda-feira (often 2a)*
Tuesday *terca-feira (often 3a)*
Wednesday *quarta-feira (often 4a)*
Thursday *quinta-feira (often 5a)*
Friday *sexta-feira (often 6a)*
Saturday *sábado*
Sunday *domingo*

Numbers

1 *um*
2 *dois*
3 *três*
4 *quatro*
5 *cinco*
6 *seis*
7 *sete*
8 *oito*
9 *nove*
10 *dez*
11 *onze*
12 *doze*
13 *treze*
14 *quatorze*
15 *quinze*
16 *dezesseis*
17 *dezessete*
18 *dezoito*
19 *dezenove*
20 *vinte*
21 *vinte um*
30 *trinta*
40 *quarenta*
50 *cinquenta*
60 *sessenta*
70 *setenta*
80 *oitenta*
90 *noventa*
100 *cem*
1,000 *mil*

Lea Garcia in Orfeu Negro

BOOKS AND FILM

Books

Non-fiction

Birds of Brazil, by Ber van Perlo. Brazil's bird diversity is one of the richest in the world. Here is the guide.

Brazil, by Michael Palin. A good primer, written in the same chatty style that Palin uses in the supporting 2012 TV series.

The Brazil Reader, by Robert M. Levine and John J. Crocitti (eds). The Brazil Reader offers a fascinating guide to Brazilian life, culture, and history.

A Concise History of Brazil, by Boris Fausto. Covers almost 500 years of Brazilian history.

The New Brazil, by Riordan Roett. The story of South America's largest country as it evolved from a remote Portuguese colony into a regional leader.

Brazil on the Rise: The Story of a Country Transformed, by Larry Rother. A view of Brazil from the New York Times' Rio bureau chief.

Disinherited Indians in Brazil, by Fiona Watson, Stephen Corry, and Caroline Pearce (eds). The story of Brazil's Indian population.

Fazendas: The Futebol: The Brazilian Way of Life, by Alex Bellos. Entertaining combination of history and anecdote that will fascinate those who have an interest in soccer.

The Lost City of Z, by David Grann. Journalist David Grann interweaves the stories of Fawcett's quest for 'Z' with his own journey into the jungle.

Ninety-Two Days: A Journey in Guiana and Brazil, by Evelyn Waugh. Waugh chronicles a South American journey in 1932.

Oscar Niemeyer: Curves of Irreverence, by Styliane Philippou. A look at the work of Brazil's greatest architect.

Rio de Janeiro, by Ruy Castro. Brazilian essayist reveals his personal Rio, with fascinating anecdotes.

Tropical Truth, by Caetano Veloso. Singer/songwriter tells how Tropicalismo revolutionized Brazilian culture as well as its politics.

Travelers' Tales Brazil, by Annette Haddad and Scott Doggett. Fifty essays on the country's commingling of cultures.

Walking the Amazon: 860 Days. One Step at Time, by Ed Stafford. Ed Stafford set off to become the first man ever to walk the entire length of the Amazon.

Fiction

Brazil, by John Updike. In the dream-Brazil of John Updike's imagining, almost anything is possible if you are young and in love.

City of the Beasts, by Isabel Allende. A coming-of-age tale set in the Amazon jungle.

The slum gang from City of God

City of God, by Paulo Lins. The novel on which the award-winning film was based: life and violence in a Rio slum.
Dom Casmurro, by Machado de Assis. A sad and darkly comic novel about love and the corrosive power of jealousy.
Dona Flor and Her Two Husbands, by Jorge Amado. One of the classics from Brazil's best-known novelist.
Elite Squad, by Luiz Eduardo Soares. The book behind the award-winning film of police corruption in Rio.
Soulstorm, by Clarice Lispector. Short stories by writer noted for her blend of suspense and romance.
Turbulence, by Chico Buarque. A nostalgic account of Rio de Janeiro.
The War of the Saints, by Jorge Amado. Another classic from Amado set in Bahia.

Film

One of the first films to use Rio is still arguably the most famous – **Flying Down to Rio** of 1933, Thornton Freeland's musical that for the first time paired Fred Astaire and Ginger Rogers. Other notable early films to use Rio include Alfred Hitchcock's 1946 World War II thriller **Notorious**, which starred Cary Grant, Ingrid Bergman and Claude Rains, and French director Marcel Camus's multi-award-winning **Orfeu Negro** (**Black Orpheus**), shot largely in the favelas of Rio and during Carnival.

More recently, Brazil was also used for the production of the James Bond blockbuster **Moonraker** (1979), Werner Herzog's **Fitzcarraldo** (1982), John Boorman's **The Emerald Forest** (1985); Roland Joffé's **The Mission** (1986); Luis Llosa's **Anaconda** (1997); John Stockwell's **Turistas** (2006); Luis Leterrier's **The Incredible Hulk** (2008) and the comedies **Moon over Parador** (1988), **Woman on Top** (2000) and **Mike Bassett: England Manager** (2001). Rio was also the backdrop for Stanley Donen's rom-com **Blame it on Rio** (1984) that starred Michael Caine and Demi Moore, in one of her first film roles.

In 2006 it was the turn of Bollywood to discover Brazil, with Sanjay Gadhavi's hit action thriller **Dhoom 2**, set in Rio de Janeiro. **CSI: Miami** has also used Rio to good effect, as did Roland Emmerich's **2012**, and the French spy spoof, **OSS117: Rio ne répond plus** (2009), by the director of **The Artist**. Sylvester Stallone used locations throughout the state of Rio for **The Expendables** (2010), as did **Fast and Furious 5: Rio Heist** (2011), and **Twilight: Breaking Dawn** (2011). Younger viewers will know the city from the animations **Rio** (2011) and **Rio 2** (2014).

Julien Temple focused on Rio for **Children of the Revolution: This is Rio**, a look at the city's music scene and history (2013).

ABOUT THIS BOOK

This *Explore Guide* has been produced by the editors of Insight Guides, whose books have set the standard for visual travel guides since 1970. With top-quality photography and authoritative recommendations, these guidebooks bring you the very best routes and itineraries in the world's most exciting destinations.

BEST ROUTES

The routes in the book provide something to suit all budgets, tastes and trip lengths. As well as covering the destination's many classic attractions, the itineraries track lesser-known sights, and there are also excursions for those who want to extend their visit outside the city. The routes embrace a range of interests, so whether you are an art fan, a gourmet, a history buff or have kids to entertain, you will find an option to suit.

We recommend reading the whole of a route before setting out. This should help you to familiarise yourself with it and enable you to plan where to stop for refreshments – options are shown in the 'Food and Drink' box at the end of each tour.

For our pick of the tours by theme, consult Recommended Routes for… (see pages 6–7).

INTRODUCTION

The routes are set in context by this introductory section, giving an overview of the destination to set the scene, plus background information on food and drink, shopping and more, while a succinct history timeline highlights the key events over the centuries.

DIRECTORY

Also supporting the routes is a Directory chapter, with a clearly organised A–Z

of practical information, our pick of where to stay while you are there and select restaurant listings; these eateries complement the more low-key cafés and restaurants that feature within the routes and are intended to offer a wider choice for evening dining. Also included here are some nightlife listings, plus a handy language guide and our recommendations for books and films about the destination.

ABOUT THE AUTHORS

Alex Corrie, who compiled the routes for this guide, is descended from Brits who moved to Brazil in the 1880s. He spent his childhood in Rio, before moving to England for school and university. After several years working with safaris and environmental conservation in East Africa, then the wine industry in Europe, Alex felt the urge to move back to Brazil. He works as a travel writer and in his spare time enjoys ocean swims, samba bars and exploring the vast country which he once again calls home.

Chris Wallace, who wrote the introduction and researched listings for this book, has been living and working in South America for over 10 years. He has authored guidebooks on Argentina, Chile, Patagonia, Colombia and Brazil.

CONTACT THE EDITORS

We hope you find this Explore Guide useful, interesting and a pleasure to read. If you have any questions or feedback on the text, pictures or maps, please do let us know. If you have noticed any errors or outdated facts, or have suggestions for places to include on the routes, we would be delighted to hear from you. Please drop us an email at hello@insightguides.com. Thanks!

CREDITS

Explore Rio de Janeiro

Editor: Rachel Lawrence
Authors: Alex Corrie, Chris Wallace
Head of Production: Rebeka Davies
Picture Editor: Tom Smyth
Cartography: original cartography Mapping Ideas Ltd, updated by Carte
Photo credits: Alamy 82, 134, 135; Belmond 94MR, 96, 97, 109; Daniel Pinheiro/BLTA 102; Gabriel Marques/ Fazenda Ponte Alta 103; Getty Images 4/5T, 24, 25, 26/27T, 37, 40, 42, 51, 52, 59L, 66/67, 78, 83, 84, 88, 89, 90, 129; iStock 7MR, 28, 34/35, 36, 50, 54, 77; Leonardo 94ML, 98, 100, 101; Photoshot 92T; PortoBay Rio Internacional 94ML, 94/95T, 99; Robert Harding 32, 91, 93; Shutterstock 7T, 26MR, 31, 34, 43, 49, 79, 80/81, 85, 92B, 119, 128; Yadid Levy/ Apa Publications 1, 4ML, 4MC, 4MR, 4MR, 4MC, 4ML, 6TL, 6MC, 6ML, 6BC, 7MR, 7M, 8ML, 8MC, 8ML, 8MC, 8MR, 8MR, 8/9T, 10, 11, 12, 13L, 12/13, 14/15, 16, 17L, 16/17, 18, 19L, 18/19, 20, 20/21, 22, 23L, 22/23, 26ML, 26MC, 26ML, 26MC, 26MR, 29L, 28/29, 30, 33, 35L, 38/39, 41, 44, 45L, 44/45, 46B, 46T, 47, 48, 53, 55, 56, 57L, 56/57, 58, 58/59, 60, 61, 62, 63L, 62/63, 64, 65, 68, 69, 70, 71L, 70/71, 72, 73, 74, 75L, 74/75, 76, 86/87, 94MC, 94MC, 94MR, 104, 105L, 104/105, 106, 107, 108, 110, 111, 112, 113, 114, 115, 116, 117, 118, 120, 121, 122, 123, 124, 125, 126/127, 130, 131, 132/133
Cover credits: Shutterstock (main) iStock (BL)

Printed by CTPS – China

All Rights Reserved
© 2016 Apa Digital (CH) AG and
Apa Publications (UK) Ltd

First Edition 2016

No part of this book may be reproduced, stored in a retrieval system or transmitted in any form or means electronic, mechanical, photocopying, recording or otherwise, without prior written permission from Apa Publications.

Every effort has been made to provide accurate information in this publication, but changes are inevitable. The publisher cannot be responsible for any resulting loss, inconvenience or injury.

DISTRIBUTION

UK, Ireland and Europe
Apa Publications (UK) Ltd
sales@insightguides.com
United States and Canada
Ingram Publisher Services
ips@ingramcontent.com
Southeast Asia
Woodslane
info@woodslane.com.au
Australia and New Zealand
Apa Publications (Singapore) Pte
singaporeoffice@insightguides.com
Hong Kong, Taiwan and China
Apa Publications (HK) Ltd
hongkongoffice@insightguides.com
Worldwide
Apa Publications (UK) Ltd
sales@insightguides.com

SPECIAL SALES, CONTENT LICENSING AND COPUBLISHING

Insight Guides can be purchased in bulk quantities at discounted prices. We can create special editions, personalised jackets and corporate imprints tailored to your needs.
sales@insightguides.com
www.insightguides.biz

INDEX

A

addresses **116**
age restrictions **116**
Amsterdam Sauer Museum **75**
architecture **10**
Arco do Teles **57**
Arcos da Lapa **44, 64**
Arpoador **73**
Avenida Mem de Sá **64**
Avenida Presidente Vargas **58**

B

Biblioteca Nacional **62**
books **134**
Botafogo **50**
budgeting for your trip **116**

C

Câmara Municipal do Rio de Janeiro **62**
Caminho dos Pescadores **69**
carnival **11**
Casa França-Brasil **58**
Casa Granado **57**
Centro Cultural Banco do Brasil **58**
Centro Cultural Correios **57**
Centro de Estudos de Pessoal **68**
Chácara do Céu **46**
Chafariz do Mestre Valentim **56**
children **117**
Cinelândia **61**
Cinema Odeon **65**
climate **12**

clothing **117**
Cobal do Humaitá **54**
Cocoruto **29**
Complexo do Alemão favelas **79**
Convento de Santo Antônio **63**
Copacabana Beach **69**
Copacabana Fort **71**
Copacabana Palace Hotel **70**
Corcovado **33**
crime and safety **118**
Cristo Redentor **35**
customs regulations **118**

D

disabled travelers **118**
Dois Irmãos **73**
Dorival Caymmi statue **70**

E

economy **15**
electricity **119**
emergencies **119**
Escadaria Selarón **65**
Estação do Bonde **44**
Estação do Trem do Corcovado **33**
etiquette **119**

F

favelas **52**
Feira de São Cristóvão (Feira Nordestina) **82**
Feira Hippie **73**
festivals **120**

film **135**
Flamengo Sports Club **76**
Floresta da Tijuca **35**
food and drink **16**
Forte do Leme **67**

G

gay and lesbian travelers **120**
geography **10**
Guanabara Bay **89**

H

health and medical care **121**
history **10, 24**
hotels
   Belmond Copacabana Palace **98**
   Byblos **103**
   Cama e Café **97**
   Casa Cool Beans **97**
   Casas Brancas **103**
   Che Lagarto **98**
   Copa Hostel **98**
   Everest Rio Hotel **100**
   Excelsior **98**
   Fasano **100**
   Fazenda Arvoredo **103**
   Fazenda Ponte Alta **103**
   Hibiscus Beach **103**
   Hotel Atlântica Praia **98**
   Hotel Caesar Park **100**
   Hotel Golden Tulip Regente **98**
   Hotel Rio Othon Palace **99**
   Hotel Santa Teresa **97**
   Hotel Vila Galé Eco

Resort **102**
Ipanema Plaza **100**
JW Marriott **99**
Lapa Hostel **96**
Leblon Spot Design
   Hostel **101**
Le Relais La Borie **103**
Marina All Suites **101**
Miramar Hotel by
   Windsor **99**
Pestana Angra **102**
Pestana Rio Atlântica **99**
Porto Bay Rio
   Internacional **99**
Pousada do Martin
   Pescodar **103**
Pousada do Ouro **102**
Pousada Porto Imperial
   102
Praia Ipanema & Best
   Western Plus Sol
   Ipanema **101**
Royal Tulip Rio **101**
Sheraton Barra Hotel &
   Suites **102**
Sheraton Rio Hotel &
   Towers **101**
Sofitel Rio **99**
Windsor Atlantica Hotel
   100
Windsor Guanabara
   Palace **96**
Windsor Hotel Florida **97**
hours and holidays **122**

I

Igreja de Nossa Senhora da
   Candelária **58**
Igreja de Nossa Senhora da
   Lapa dos Mercadores **57**

Igreja de São Francisco **63**
Igreja e Mosteiro de São
   Bento **59**
internet facilities **122**
Ipanema **73**
Ipanema Beach **73**

J

Jardim Botânico **38**

L

Lagoa Rodrigo de Freitas **76**
Lagoon **76**
language **130**
Lapa **64**
Largo do Boticário **37**
Largo do Curvelo **45**
Largo dos Guimarães **47**
layout **10**
Leblon Beach **75**
Leme Beach **69**
local customs **15**

M

Maracanã **80**
media **122**
money **122**
Morro da Urca **29**
Museu Casa de Rui Barbosa
   50
Museu de Arte do Rio (MAR)
   60
Museu do Amanhã **59**
Museu do Índio **53**
Museu do Meio Ambiente
   40
Museu Internacional de Arte
   Naïf **36**

Museu Nacional de Belas
   Artes **63**
Museu Villa-Lobos **51**

N

Niterói **83**
   Adão e Eva **88**
   Charitas **87**
   Fortaleza de Santa Cruz
      88
   Jurujuba **87**
   Museu de Arte
      Contemporânea **86**
   Palácio dos Correios
      85
   Praça Araribóia **85**
   Praça Quinze in Rio's
      Centro **83, 85**
   Praia de Icaraí **86**
   Praia de São Francisco
      87
   Praia do Ingá **86**
   São Francisco de Xavier
      church **87**

O

Our Lady of the Conception
   grotto **31**

P

Paço Imperial **56**
Paineiras station **35**
Paquetá Island **89**
   Cemitério dos Pássaros
      92
   Estação das Barcas **91**
   Parque Darke de Mattos
      92

Pedra da Moreninha **92**
Praça Quinze de
    Novembro **90**
Praia da Moreninha **92**
Praia de Catimbau **93**
Praia de São Roque **92**
Praia do Lameirão **93**
Praia dos Tamoios **93**
Praia José Bonifácio **92**
Parque das Ruinas **45**
Parque Lage **77**
people **12**
Pista Claudio Coutinho **31**
politics **15**
post **123**
Praça Corumbá **53**
Praça General Osório **73**
Praça General Tibúrcio **30**
Praça Nossa Senhora da
    Paz **75**
Praça Quinze **56**
Praia Vermelha **30**

R

religion **123**
restaurants
    Adega do Pimenta **48**
    Al Kuwait **65**
    Amarelinho **65, 106**
    Antiquarius **111**
    Aprazível **112**
    Armazém São Thiago
        113
    Assis **37**
    Atrium **106**
    Azumi **107**
    Bar Brasil **65, 106**
    Bar da Tia Leleta **93**
    Bar do Arnaudo **48**
    Bar do Gengibre **60**

Bar do Horto **43**
Bar do Mineiro **48**
Bar do Oswaldo **104**
Bar Lagoa **111**
Bar Luiz **106**
Bar Urca **113**
Bistrô Plage **77**
Bracarense **111**
Brasileirinho **107**
Bráz **110**
Café 18 do Forte **71**
Café Lamas **108**
Cais do Oriente **106**
Casa de Artes de
    Paquetá **93**
Casa de Feijoada **109**
Catarina Doces e
    Salgados **54**
Cedro do Líbano **106**
Celeiro **112**
Cipriani **108**
Confeitaria Colombo **107**
Cota 200
    Restaurante **32**
Couveflor **110**
Espírito do Chopp **54**
Fasano al Mare **109**
Filé de Ouro **111**
Flor da Urca **113**
Fogo de Chão **105**
Garota da Urca **113**
Garota de Ipanema **77**
Gero **109**
Giuseppe Grill **112**
Goya Beira **113**
Gula Gula **110**
Hachiko **107**
Hansl **105**
Hipódromo **43**
Intihuasi **108**
Irajá **106**

Joaquina Bar e
    Restaurante **54**
Jobi **112**
Ki **111**
La Bicyclette **43**
La Botticella **105**
Laguna **105**
Le Pré Catelan **108**
Luna Café **37**
Mamma Rosa **37**
Manoel & Juaquim **110**
Marius Degustare **108**
Mocellín **88**
Nativo **105**
New Natural **110**
Nói **88**
Olympe **111**
Palaphita Kitch **111**
Pe'ahi **105**
Pérgula Restaurant **71**
Pizzaria Guanabara
    112
Plataforma **112**
Prado **43**
Restaurante Berbigão
    88
Restaurante Mauá **60**
Restaurante Paz e Amor
    77
Rio Minho **107**
Rotisseria Sirio Libanesa
    109
Rubaiyat Rio **43**
Rústico Bar e
    Restaurante **48**
Satyricon **110**
Tacacá do Norte **109**
Terra Brasilis **32**
The Line Bistro **60**
Rio Scenarium **64**
Rua do Ouvidor **57**

Rua Vinícius de Moraes 75

S

Santa Marta funicular 54
Santa Teresa 44
São Sebastião Metropolitan Cathedral 64
shopping 20
smoking 124
Sugarloaf 28
Sugarloaf Mountain 29

T

Teleférico do Complexo do Alemão 78
telephones 124
Theatro Municipal do Rio de Janeiro 62
time zones 125
toilets 125
tourist information 125
tours and guides 125
transportation 126
Travessa do Comércio 57

V

Vidigal 73
visas and passports 129

W

weights and measures 129
women travelers 129

Z

Zona Norte 78

MAP LEGEND

●	Start of tour	🅜	Museum/gallery	⚑	Beach
→	Tour & route direction	📖	Library	✳	Viewpoint
❶	Recommended sight	🎭	Theatre	2713△	Altitude in m
❷	Recommended restaurant/café	✚	Hospital		Important building
★	Place of interest	✦	Police		Hotel
❶	Tourist information	⌖†	Church		Urban area
✉	Post office	🚌	Main bus station		Park
🛉	Statue/monument	🅟	Car park	† †	Cemetery
		✈	Airport		Pedestrian area
		Ⓜ	Subway		Non-urban area

INSIGHTGUIDES.COM

ght Guides website offers a unique way to plan and boo
ips online. Be inspired by our curated destination conte
ly travel blog and build your own dream trip from our ra
customisable experiences, created by our local experts

t our homepage and be inspired by our selection of fascina
travel stories, stunning photography and lively blogs.

hoose your dream trip from our carefully selected range o
destinations, devised by trusted local experts.

tomise your perfect trip – choose your hotel, add experien
and excursions – and book securely online.

INSIGHT ○ GUIDES

TRAVEL MADE EASY. ASK LOCAL EXPERTS